Chinese
COOKING

CLB 1669
Copyright © 1987 by Colour Library Books Ltd.
Guildford, Surrey, England.
First published in U.S.A. 1987
by Exeter Books
Distributed by Bookthrift
Exeter is a trademark of Bookthrift Marketing, Inc.
Bookthrift is a registered trademark of Bookthrift Marketing, Inc.
New York, New York
ALL RIGHTS RESERVED
ISBN 0-671-08255-8
Printed and bound in Barcelona, Spain by Cronión, S.A.

COMPILED AND EDITED BY
Delia Clarke
RECIPES WRITTEN BY
Lalita Ahmed, Judith Ferguson and Carolyn Garner
PHOTOGRAPHED BY
Peter Barry
DESIGNED BY
Philip Clucas MSIAD
PRODUCED BY
David Gibbon, Gerald Hughes and Ted Smart

Chinese COOKING

Exeter Books

NEW YORK

CONTENTS

Introduction page 5

Soups and Appetizers page 8

Rice, Noodles and Eggs page 30

Fish and Seafood page 46

Meat Dishes page 68

Poultry Recipes page 114

Vegetables and Sauces page 142

Desserts page 164

Glossary page 170

Index page 174

INTRODUCTION

As in many other countries so in China, the preparation and sharing of a meal are of great social and family importance. Mealtimes are when the whole family as well as friends gather together to share food as well as experiences, happiness and problems. To the Chinese, therefore, the meal is about more than just eating and satisfying a physical need, it is an integral and important part of their social life. Additionally, through cooking itself one demonstrates personal inventiveness and creativity, as well as one's cultural background, so cooking can always be seen as a pleasurable activity.

In Chinese cuisine, the preparation of the food is of paramount importance. Many dishes require very fine chopping and shredding of the various ingredients, and these are normally combined in a very orderly manner. Those ingredients which are not easily available in the Western world can generally be substituted. Many Chinese recipes, of course, feature ingredients so exotic that they cannot be found in the West, and these have been avoided in this book, whilst others have been included which, whilst not necessarily authentic, reflect a Chinese influence or means of preparation.

The main cooking technique used to produce good Chinese food is stir-frying. A wok is ideal, but a deep skillet will serve the purpose almost as well. The traditional wok is made of heavy-gauge carbon steel which conducts heat well, giving a quick high temperature. However, this medium will rust if not oiled and given proper care. Lengthy cooking in liquid may impart a metallic taste to the food, or may cause the discoloration of white liquids or food. Aluminium and stainless steel woks are also available and are a good choice, particularly if steaming, braising, boiling, or cooking for a long time. These woks need no seasoning, but do not heat as efficiently as carbon steel.

Stir-frying is a fuel and time saver and is unique to wok cooking, where small pieces of food are toss-cooked in minutes over intense heat in a very small amount of oil. The shape of the wok allows for tossing with abandon. Food is cooked in a matter of minutes and the flavors and juices remain sealed in, resulting in succulent meat, poultry and seafood, and tender and crisp vegetables. Nutritional values are retained, as are the fresh, bright colors of the vegetables.

Stir-frying requires good temperature control, and this is easily learnt with practice. The wok or pan should be heated, then the temperature reduced before adding the oil. If the utensil is too hot the oil will burn, giving a charred, oily taste to the food, which may burn, too. The heat should be progressively raised for the addition of other ingredients. All ingredients should be prepared and at hand before beginning to cook, and this includes any sauces or seasonings. Meat and poultry should be very thinly and evenly sliced, and ingredients that take the longest time to cook should be put into the wok first. Add small amounts of food at a time, in batches if necessary. Once cooked, the food must be served and eaten immediately.

Chinese food incorporates six basic flavors: sweet, sour, salty, spicy, pungent and hot. The use of these flavors and their respective proportions must be well balanced. Flavoring is always supplemented by ready-prepared sauces, the most essential of which is soy sauce. Others commonly used are plum and oyster sauces.

As in so much that is Oriental, presentation is every bit as important as the preparation. After all, what appeals to the eye also appeals to the mind, and thence to the heart and stomach. A slice of cleverly carved carrot, a thin sliver of tomato and cleverly arranged parsley or coriander can add that all-important dash of color.

Garnishes for Chinese dishes tend to be very simple. The following two are quite easy to "create", and can be prepared in advance:

Chili Flowers Choose small red or green chili peppers. Cut into thin strips, lengthwise, to within ½-1 inch of the stem. Keep the stem end intact and carefully remove the seeds and core. Place in iced water for several hours or overnight until the "petals" open up. Eat at your own risk!

Green Onion Brushes Trim the onions into 3-4 inch lengths. Cut the greener end into thin strips and leave the white "bulb" end intact. Alternatively, cut both ends into thin strips, leaving ½ inch of the middle intact. Soak as for chili flowers.

Although the microwave oven could be considered anathema to Chinese cooking, it adapts surprisingly well and many Chinese specialties are possible with a microwave oven. The usual cornstarch-based Chinese sauces need more thickening because liquids evaporate less in a microwave, but otherwise they are easy to prepare. Stir-frying transfers successfully from the wok to the browning dish, and you can even achieve a stir-fried effect without one. The microwave section of this book features recipes prepared in a 700W oven. If using ovens of a different maximum power output, the following conversion can be used as a rough guide:

For **500W** ovens, add 40 seconds for each minute stated in the recipe.

For **600W** ovens, add 20 seconds for each minute stated in the recipe.

For **650W** ovens, you will only need to allow a slight increase in the cooking time over the 700W model.

 Recipes featuring this symbol in the heading have been specially adapted for microwave preparation.

SOUPS AND APPETIZERS

Chicken Corn Soup with Almonds

PREPARATION TIME: 15 minutes

MICROWAVE COOKING TIME: 5-8 minutes

SERVES: 4 people

2 8oz cans creamed corn
4 cups chicken stock
2 chicken breasts, finely chopped
2 tbsps cornstarch
2 tbsps rice wine
½ cup toasted almonds
Salt and pepper

Combine corn, stock and chicken in a large, deep bowl. Partially cover and cook 3-5 minutes or until chicken is nearly cooked. Combine rice wine, cornstarch and stir into the soup. Cook 2-3 minutes to allow cornstarch to thicken and clear. Sprinkle with toasted almonds and serve.

Stuffed Mushrooms with Pork and Water Chestnuts

PREPARATION TIME: 30 minutes

MICROWAVE COOKING TIME: 4 minutes per batch

SERVES: 4 people

12 dried Chinese mushrooms
4oz ground pork
2 water chestnuts, finely chopped
1 stick celery, finely chopped
2 tsps soy sauce
1 tsp oyster sauce
Salt and pepper

GARNISH
4 green onions, sliced

Soak the mushrooms in hot water for 30 minutes. Mix all the remaining ingredients. Drain the mushrooms

This page: Stuffed Mushrooms with Pork and Water Chestnuts. Facing page: Chicken Corn Soup with Almonds (top) and Soup of Mushrooms and Peas (page 10) (bottom).

and reserve ½ cup of the soaking water. Pat the mushrooms dry on paper towels and cut off the stems. Combine remaining ingredients and fill the mushrooms with the pork mixture, smoothing out with a knife. Place the mushrooms in 1 layer in a shallow dish, stuffing-side up. Pour around the soaking water and cover the dish with pierced plastic wrap. Cook on HIGH for 4 minutes. Baste occasionally with the mushroom liquid. Transfer the mushrooms to a serving dish and sprinkle with the onions. Serve hot.

Soup of Mushrooms and Peas

PREPARATION TIME: 15 minutes

MICROWAVE COOKING TIME: 10 minutes

SERVES: 4 people

12 dried Chinese mushrooms, soaked 30 minutes
4oz ham, shredded
4 cups light stock
1 tbsp light soy sauce
2 cups fresh peas
Salt and pepper

Remove the stems and slice the mushrooms finely. Combine with the remaining ingredients and cook 10 minutes on HIGH or until peas are just tender.

Hot and Sour Soup

PREPARATION TIME: 20 minutes

COOKING TIME: 7-8 minutes

SERVES: 6-8 people

6¼ cups chicken broth
½ cup lean pork, shredded, or cubed barbecued pork
½ cup peeled de-veined shrimp
1oz bamboo shoots, sliced
2 cloud ear fungus, soaked in boiling water for 5 minutes and chopped
2-3 green onions, chopped
Salt to taste
1 tbsp fine granulated sugar

½ tsp monosodium glutamate (optional)
1 tsp dark soy sauce
½ tsp light soy sauce
1½ tbsps vinegar
1 tsp chili oil or chili sauce
¼ tsp sesame oil
½ tsp Shao Hsing wine (optional)
1 egg, well beaten
1 tbsp cornstarch
2 tbsps water

Mix broth with pork, shrimp, and all the remaining ingredients except the well beaten egg, cornstarch and water. Simmer gently for 4-5 minutes. Remove from heat and add the egg, stirring gently, until the egg forms 'threads' in the soup. Blend the cornstarch with the water and add to the soup. Simmer for 1 minute until the soup thickens and serve immediately.

Chicken Noodle Soup

PREPARATION TIME: 10 minutes

COOKING TIME: 10-12 minutes

SERVES: 8 people

1lb Shanghai noodles, or very thin noodles
2 tbsps salad or olive oil
2 cups cooked chicken, cubed
2 cups Chinese white cabbage or ordinary white cabbage, shredded
6¼ cups chicken broth

SEASONING
½ tsp fine granulated sugar
½ tsp salt
2 tsps Shao Hsing wine (optional)
½ tsp monosodium glutamate
2 tsps light soy sauce

Add the noodles to a large pan of boiling water. Stir to loosen the bundles and boil for 4-5 minutes. (The noodles should be just tender but not overcooked.) Drain noodles well. Meanwhile, heat the oil in the wok and fry the chicken for 1-2 minutes. Remove the chicken and then fry the cabbage in the same oil for 2 minutes. Add the seasoning ingredients and stir-fry for 1 minute. Add the chicken and cook for a further 1-2 minutes until the cabbage is tender. Add the broth and

bring to the boil. Divide noodles among 6-8 warm soup bowls and add the hot soup. Serve immediately.

Chinese Parsley and Fish Soup

PREPARATION TIME: 10 minutes

COOKING TIME: 7-8 minutes

SERVES: 6 people

1lb whitefish fillet, cut into 6 even-sized pieces
4 cups chicken broth
½ inch fresh root ginger, peeled and thinly sliced
Salt to taste
Freshly ground black pepper to taste
Pinch monosodium glutamate (optional)
2 green onions, finely chopped
½ tsp cornstarch
2 sprigs Chinese parsley, finely chopped
18-20 thin cucumber slices

Wash fish in cold water and gently simmer in chicken broth for 2-3 minutes. Remove the fish pieces carefully. Add ginger, salt, pepper, MSG and onion and simmer the stock for 2-3 minutes. Strain. Dissolve cornstarch in 1 tbsp of water or cold broth and add to the soup. Simmer for 2 minutes until the soup thickens. Add fish pieces and bring back to the boil. Serve in soup bowls, sprinkled with chopped parsley and cucumber slices.

Duck Soup

PREPARATION TIME: 10 minutes

COOKING TIME: 8 minutes

SERVES: 6 people

2 green onions, finely chopped
1 tbsp cooked oil, or salad or olive oil
1 inch fresh root ginger, peeled and finely chopped

Facing page: Chicken Noodle Soup (top), Hot and Sour Soup (center left) and Chinese Parsley and Fish Soup (bottom).

1 cup cooked duck meat, chopped
1 large wedge winter melon, peeled and
    thinly sliced
6¼ cups chicken broth
Salt to taste
Pinch monosodium glutamate (optional)
1 tbsp Shao Hsing wine or dry sherry
    (optional)
1 tsp cornstarch blended with 1 tbsp broth
Freshly ground black pepper to taste

Fry the onions in the oil for 1 minute.
Add ginger and duck meat. Stir-fry for
1 minute. Add winter melon and stir-
fry for a further 1-2 minutes and then
add broth and the remaining
ingredients. Gently simmer for 2-3
minutes until the soup becomes clear.
Serve immediately.

Steamed Open Dumplings

PREPARATION TIME: 1 hour	
COOKING TIME: 10-15 minutes	
MAKES: 24	

FILLING
1 cup medium size peeled shrimp, finely
    chopped
1½ cups ground pork or beef
2 black mushrooms, soaked and finely
    chopped
Salt to taste
½ tsp brown sugar

SEASONING
½ tsp monosodium glutamate (optional)
1 tbsp cornstarch
1½ tsps dark soy sauce
1 tsp light soy sauce
¼ tsp freshly ground black pepper
1 tbsp sesame oil
24 wonton wrappers

Mix the ground pork, shrimp,
mushrooms, salt and sugar together.
Add the seasoning ingredients and mix
well. Allow to stand for 30 minutes.
Take each wonton wrapper and spoon
a little filling in the center. Fold up the
edges around the filling but do not
completely enclose it. (An open ended
dumpling is produced with the sides of
the wrapper gathered around the
filling.) Flatten the base by pressing it
slightly so that it will stand upright in a
steamer. Grease an ordinary steamer or
a bamboo steamer and arrange the
dumplings in it. Steam for 15-20
minutes. Serve hot with a dip.

Chicken and Mushroom Soup

PREPARATION TIME: 20 minutes	
COOKING TIME: 6-8 minutes	
SERVES: 6 people	

1 cup small cap mushrooms, sliced
⅓ cup dried brown mushrooms, soaked
    and then sliced
⅓ cup dried black mushrooms, soaked
    and then sliced
1 tbsp salad or olive oil
6¼ cups chicken broth
1 cup shredded cooked chicken
3 green onions, finely chopped
¼ tsp monosodium glutamate (optional)
Salt to taste
1 tbsp light soy sauce
2 tsps Shao Hsing wine (optional)
Pinch ground white pepper
1 tsp cornstarch blended with 1 tbsp broth

Stir-fry the mushrooms in the oil for 2
minutes and then remove them. Bring
the broth to the boil in a large pan with
the remaining ingredients, apart from
the cornstarch and mushrooms, and
simmer for 3-4 minutes. Add the
blended cornstarch and the
mushrooms, and simmer for 1-2
minutes. Serve immediately.

Wonton Soup

PREPARATION TIME: 10 minutes	
COOKING TIME: 8 minutes	
SERVES: 6 people	

20-24 wontons
2 sprigs Chinese parsley, or watercress,
    finely chopped
6¼ cups chicken broth
2-3 green onions, finely chopped
1 inch fresh root ginger, peeled and finely
    chopped
Salt to taste
1 tbsp soy sauce
Pinch monosodium glutamate (optional)
½ tsp fine granulated sugar
Few drops sesame oil
¼ tsp ground white pepper

Boil wontons in a large saucepan of
water for 2-3 minutes until they float
to the surface. Remove and drain.
Divide cooked wontons and parsley
among 6-8 soup bowls. Bring broth to

boil and add onions, ginger, salt and
the remaining ingredients. Cook for 2-
3 minutes, pour over the wontons and
serve immediately.

Steamed Shrimp Pancakes

PREPARATION TIME: 1 hour	
COOKING TIME: 10-15 minutes	
MAKES: 25-30	

1½ cups all-purpose flour or high gluten
    flour
1½ tbsps cornstarch
¼ tsp salt
1 tbsp salad or olive oil
3 tbsps beaten egg
2 tbsps water
2 tbsps all-purpose flour mixed with cold
    water to a smooth paste

**Duck Soup (page 10) (top),
Chicken and Mushroom Soup
(center right) and Wonton
Soup (right).**

FILLING
1½ cups peeled shrimp, finely chopped
2 green onions, bulb only, finely chopped
¼ tsp salt, or to taste
1 tsp cornstarch to bind

Sift the flour, cornstarch and salt into a bowl. Add the oil, beaten egg and water and mix to make a stiff dough. Leave for 30 minutes to rest. Knead well for 5-6 minutes and roll into 25-30 6 inch circles on wax paper. To make the filling, mix all the ingredients except the cornstarch together, and then bind with the cornstarch. Place the filling in the center of each pancake and flatten. Spread flour and water paste around the edge of each pancake and fold up

from one end to make a roll. Arrange the pancakes in a greased ordinary or Chinese bamboo steamer and cook over boiling water for 10-15 minutes. Serve piping hot with chili or soy sauce dip.

ALTERNATIVE
To make rice pancakes, soak 4oz rice for 10 minutes. Grind with water to make a very fine paste of batter consistency. Add 1 tbsp oil and mix well. Line a steamer with fine muslin and spoon in a little batter; spread it out into a thin pancake. Steam for 5 minutes. Place a little filling on the pancake and roll up. Steam for 10 minutes and serve piping hot with a dip.

Facing page: **Four Happiness Dumplings (page 16) (top left), Steamed Shrimp Pancakes (page 12) (bottom left) and Steamed Open Dumplings (page 12) (right). Facing page: Seafood Hot and Sour Soup (top) and Corn and Chicken Soup (bottom).**

Corn and Chicken Soup

PREPARATION TIME: 15 minutes

COOKING TIME: 45 minutes

SERVES: 4 people

1 chicken, with giblets
1 8oz can cream style corn
1 onion, peeled and chopped roughly

1 carrot, scraped and chopped roughly
1 stick celery, chopped
6 peppercorns
Parsley stalks
1 bay leaf
5 cups water
Salt
Pepper

GARNISH
Chopped parsley or chives

Clean chicken, and cut into quarters. Put into wok with giblets, chopped vegetables, peppercorns, bay leaf, parsley stalks, seasoning and water. Bring to the boil. Reduce heat and simmer for 30 minutes. Strain and return stock to wok. Remove meat from chicken and cut into fine shreds. Add undrained corn to stock, and bring to boil. Simmer for 5 minutes. Add chicken and cook for 1 minute. Sprinkle with chopped parsley or chives. Serve hot.

Seafood Hot and Sour Soup

PREPARATION TIME: 20 minutes

COOKING TIME: 20 minutes

SERVES: 4 people

2 dried Chinese mushrooms
1 cake fresh beancurd, diced
4oz shrimp, shelled and de-veined
2½ cups light stock, preferably fish stock
½ cup crab meat, or 2 crab-sticks, cut into ½" slices
1 tbsp oyster sauce
1 tbsp light soy sauce
1 tbsp lemon juice
½ tsp lemon rind, cut into slivers
1 tbsp vegetable oil
1 red chili pepper, seeds removed, and finely sliced
2 green onions, sliced
Salt
Pepper
1 tsp sesame oil

GARNISH
Fresh coriander, if desired

Soak mushrooms in hot water and set aside for 20 minutes. Heat wok, add vegetable oil and, when hot, stir-fry shrimp, chili pepper, lemon rind and green onions. Add stock, oyster sauce and light soy sauce, and bring to the boil. Reduce heat and simmer for 5 minutes. Add salt and pepper to taste. Remove hard stalks from mushrooms and slice caps finely. Add crab meat, beancurd and Chinese mushrooms to wok, and cook a further 5 minutes. Stir in lemon juice and sesame oil. Adjust seasoning, and serve sprinkled with fresh coriander leaves if desired.

Chili Shrimp

PREPARATION TIME: 10-15 minutes
MICROWAVE COOKING TIME: 4½-5½ minutes
SERVES: 4 people

1lb jumbo shrimp
2 tbsps oil
2 cloves garlic, crushed
2 tbsps chili sauce (hot or sweet)
1 tbsp rice wine
1 tbsp lemon juice
Salt

GARNISH
Chili pepper flowers

Remove the heads and shells of the shrimp, but leave on the very ends of the tails. Wash, de-vein and pat dry. Put the oil and garlic into a bowl and cover with plastic wrap. Cook on HIGH 1 minute. Stir in the chili sauce, wine, lemon juice and salt. Cook 30 seconds on HIGH. Add the shrimp and cook for 3-4 minutes on MEDIUM. Serve hot or cold.

Four Happiness Dumplings

PREPARATION TIME: 30-45 minutes for pastry; 20-30 minutes for filling
COOKING TIME: 20 minutes
MAKES: 30-35

PASTRY
1¾ cups all-purpose flour
Pinch of salt
1 cup boiling water

Put the flour and salt into a bowl. Add the boiling water and mix quickly to make a dough. Cover and allow to stand for 20-30 minutes. Knead the dough for 2-3 minutes, sprinkling the work surface with a little cornstarch if needed. Divide the dough into 30-35 equal portions and roll each one to a circle 2½ inches in diameter.

FILLING
1½ cups ground lean pork
2 black mushrooms, soaked and diced
½ cup finely chopped mixed vegetables (peas, carrots, celery, etc.)
½ tsp brown sugar or maple syrup
2½ tsps light soy sauce
¼ tsp freshly ground black pepper
1 egg
5-6 chives, finely chopped
Salt to taste
1 tbsp salad or olive oil
1½ tsps cornstarch
2 tbsps all-purpose flour mixed with a little cold water to a smooth paste

Mix the pork with the mushrooms, mixed vegetables, sugar, soy sauce, black pepper, egg, chives and salt to taste. Add the oil and cornstarch and mix well with a fork. Divide filling into 30 to 35 equal portions. Fill each dumpling wrapper with a portion of filling and shape into crescent-shaped dumplings. Steam them in an ordinary steamer or a Chinese bamboo steamer for about 20 minutes. Serve with a dip and chili sauce. To make the crescent shape, place a wrapper on a flat surface, put a little filling in the center, spread the edges with a little flour and water paste and pinch the edges of the wrapper together to seal. Pull one corner of the filled wonton around and over the other corner. Press to seal.

Garlic Shrimp with Salt and Pepper

PREPARATION TIME: 10-15 minutes
MICROWAVE COOKING TIME: 4½-5½ minutes
SERVES: 4 people

1lb jumbo shrimp
2 tbsps oil
2 cloves garlic, minced
3 tbsps oyster sauce
2 tbsps soy sauce
1 tbsp lemon juice
2 tsp coarsely ground black pepper
Salt

GARNISH
Green onion brushes

Prepare the shrimp as for Chili Shrimp. Put the oil and garlic into a bowl. Cover and cook 1 minute on HIGH. Add the oyster sauce, soy sauce, lemon juice and cook 30 seconds on HIGH. Stir in the shrimp and cook for 3-4 minutes on MEDIUM. Sprinkle with salt and pepper before serving. Garnish with green onion brushes (see introduction).

Chinese Noodle Soup with Pork Dumplings

PREPARATION TIME: 20 minutes
MICROWAVE COOKING TIME: 10 minutes plus 1 minute standing time
SERVES: 4 people

8oz ground pork
½ tsp ground ginger
1 tbsp cornstarch
2 tbsps light soy sauce
4 cups stock
¼ package thin Chinese noodles
1 tbsp rice wine
4 green onions, sliced

Mix the cornstarch with the soy sauce. Combine with the pork and ginger. Shape into small balls. Heat the stock 5 minutes on HIGH in a large, deep bowl. Add the pork balls and cook 2 minutes on HIGH. Add the noodles and wine and cook a further 3 minutes on HIGH. Add the green onions and leave to stand 1 minute before serving.

Facing page: Garlic Shrimp with Salt and Pepper (top) and Chili Shrimp (bottom).

20 minutes. Remove and discard stems. Slice mushroom caps thinly. Soak noodles in boiling salted water for 2 minutes. Rinse in cold water. Drain. Slice chicken finely. Heat wok and add peanut oil. Add garlic and ginger, and fry gently for 5 minutes, then discard. Add chicken, and fry for a few minutes until meat has turned white. Add mushrooms, shallots, cabbage and stock. Bring to the boil and simmer for 5 minutes. Gradually pour in eggs and stir so that they cook in shreds. Mix cornstarch with 1 tbsp of water, and pour into soup, stirring continuously. Cook for 2 minutes or until soup thickens. Add noodles, soy sauce and sherry. Serve immediately.

Corn and Crabmeat Soup

PREPARATION TIME: 10 minutes

MICROWAVE COOKING TIME: 4 minutes plus 5 minutes standing time

SERVES: 4 people

2 8oz cans creamed corn
1 onion
4 cups chicken stock
1 small piece ginger root, peeled and grated
1 tsp sherry
2 tbsps cornstarch
8oz crabmeat
2 green onions
Salt

Combine the onion and corn in a deep bowl. Cover and cook 1 minute on HIGH to soften onion slightly. Add the ginger, sherry, stock and cornstarch mixed with 2 tbsps water. Cook for 2-3 minutes until thickened, stirring halfway through cooking. Stir in the crabmeat, reserving about 2 tbsps for garnish.

Chinese Combination Soup

PREPARATION TIME: 30 minutes

COOKING TIME: 20 minutes

SERVES: 4 people

4 dried Chinese mushrooms
8oz chicken
4oz fine/thread egg noodles
1 clove garlic, sliced thinly
1 tsp finely sliced root ginger
¼ small cabbage, shredded
2½ cups chicken stock
1 tbsp peanut oil
2 eggs, beaten
1 tbsp dark soy sauce
1 tbsp sherry
1 tbsp water
1 tsp cornstarch
2 shallots, peeled and sliced finely

Soak mushrooms in hot water for

This page: Chinese Noodle Soup with Pork Dumplings (page 16) (top) and Corn and Crabmeat Soup (bottom). Facing page: Chinese Combination Soup (top) and Eggflower Soup (page 20) (bottom).

Leave to stand, covered, for 3 minutes before serving. Sprinkle reserved crabmeat and green onion on top of each serving.

Eggflower Soup

PREPARATION TIME: 10 minutes

COOKING TIME: 10 minutes

SERVES: 4 people

2½ cups chicken stock
2 eggs, lightly beaten
1 tbsp light soy sauce
1¾ cups canned plum tomatoes
2 green onions, chopped finely

Drain and chop tomatoes, removing seeds, and reserve juice. Bring soy sauce, tomato juice and stock to the boil in the wok. Add tomatoes and half the green onions, and cook for 2 minutes. Dribble beaten eggs in gradually, stirring continuously. Serve immediately, sprinkled with remaining green onions.

Steamed Crabmeat and Egg Custard

PREPARATION TIME: 30 minutes

MICROWAVE COOKING TIME: 8-9 minutes

SERVES: 4 people

2 eggs, beaten
½ cup chicken stock
1 tbsp sherry
6oz cooked crabmeat
4 chopped green onions
3 chopped water chestnuts
2 finely chopped Chinese mushrooms,
    pre-cooked 30 minutes
1 tsp grated fresh ginger root
Salt

Mix the eggs, stock, sherry and add the remaining ingredients. Spoon into lightly oiled custard cups. Cover loosely and arrange in a circle on the turntable and cook 1 minute on HIGH. Reduce to LOW/DEFROST and cook for 7-8 minutes or until softly set. Unmold onto plates and serve with soy sauce. Surround with shredded Chinese cabbage if desired.

Wonton Wrappers

PREPARATION TIME: 5-6 hours (including standing time)

MAKES: 40-50 wrappers

1 cup all-purpose flour
2 tbsps beaten egg
2 tbsps cold water
Cornstarch

Sift flour and gradually add the beaten egg and water mixed together. Mix to a stiff dough. Knead firmly for 5-6 minutes and wrap in plastic wrap. Leave to stand at room temperature for 4-5 hours. Roll out into a very large square on a work surface dusted with cornstarch. The pastry should be almost transparent. Cut into 40-50 3 inch round or square wrappers. Dust each wrapper with cornstarch before stacking. Store the wrappers, wrapped securely in plastic wrap, in the refrigerator, for up to 24 hours. If they are allowed to dry out they will split during cooking.

Spring Roll Wrappers

PREPARATION TIME: 20 minutes, plus chilling time

MAKES: 12 wrappers

1 scant cup all-purpose flour
1 egg, beaten
A little cold water

Sift the flour into a bowl. Make a well in the center and add the beaten egg and a little cold water. Mix to a soft yet firm dough, adding a little extra water if necessary. Knead the dough until it is really pliable (this helps to make the gluten work). Chill, covered, for 4 hours or overnight. Allow to come back to room temperature. Roll out the dough on a well-floured surface to about ¼ inch thick. Cut into 12 equal pieces, and then roll each piece to a square about 6x6 inches – each square should be very thin.

Right: Steamed Crabmeat and Egg Custard.

Wontons with Pork and Shrimp Filling

PREPARATION TIME: 30 minutes

COOKING TIME: 10-15 minutes

MAKES: 40-50

1½ cups lean ground pork
Salad or olive oil
1½ cups peeled small shrimp, finely
    chopped
3 green onions, finely chopped
½ tsp ground white pepper
1¼ tbsps soy sauce
1½ tsps rice wine or dry sherry
½ tsp salt, or to taste
1½ tsps cornstarch blended with 2 tbsps
    water
40-50 wonton wrappers
2 tbsps all-purpose flour, mixed with a
    little cold water to a smooth paste

Fry pork in 2 tbsps oil until it loses its
pink color. Add shrimp and onions and
fry for 3-4 minutes. Add pepper, soy
sauce and wine. Season with salt and
stir-fry for 1-2 minutes. Add the
blended cornstarch and stir over a
moderate heat until thickened. Allow
to cool before filling the wontons.
Divide filling into 40-50 equal portions.
Take a wonton wrapper, moisten the
edges with the flour and water paste.
Place a portion of filling in the center of
the wonton and gather up the edges to
make a neat round, or shape in such a
way as to make a triangle or any other
shape that you prefer. Once you have
shaped all the wontons, deep-fry them
in hot oil until crisp and golden. You
will need to fry them in 3 or more
batches. Drain well on absorbent paper
before serving.

Spring Rolls

PREPARATION TIME: 20-30 minutes

COOKING TIME: about 20 minutes

MAKES: 12

2 cups lean, raw pork or beef, finely
    shredded
1 cup small to medium, shelled shrimp
    (either uncooked or boiled)
4 green onions, finely chopped
Salad or olive oil

2 tsps fresh root ginger, peeled and
    shredded
1⅓ cups white cabbage, shredded
1-1¼ cups bean sprouts
1¼ tbsps soy sauce
Salt to taste
12 spring roll wrappers, each 6 inches
    square (see recipe)

2 tbsps all-purpose flour, mixed with a
    little cold water to a smooth paste

Fry the shredded pork and the shrimp
with the spring onions in 1 tbsp of oil
for 2-3 minutes. Add the ginger,
cabbage and bean sprouts, and stir-fry
for 2-3 minutes. Add soy sauce, and

Facing page: Fried Meat Dumplings (top right), Spring Rolls (center left) and Wontons with Pork and Shrimp Filling (bottom). Above: Crab Rolls (page 24) (top) and Rice Paper Shrimp Parcels (page 24) (bottom). Above right: Egg Drop Soup (page 24) (top), Crab and Watercress Soup (page 26) (center) and Crab and Sweet Corn Soup (page 28) (bottom).

season with a little salt if desired. Remove from the heat and allow to cool. Lay out the spring roll wrappers on a clean working surface, with one point of each wrapper facing you. Divide the filling mixture into 12 equal portions and place one portion of filling just above the front point of each wrapper. Fold in the opposite side points, so that they overlap slightly like an envelope – secure the side points with a little flour and water paste. Starting with the point facing you, roll each wrapper up around the filling, securing the remaining point with a little flour and water paste. Repeat in

exactly the same way with the remaining spring roll wrappers. They will keep a better shape if you chill them for 1 hour before cooking. Deep-fry over a medium heat until golden brown and crisp. Drain thoroughly on absorbent paper and serve hot with a selection of dips or chili sauce. The spring rolls can be frozen, uncooked.

Fried Meat Dumplings

PREPARATION TIME:	10 minutes
COOKING TIME:	about 15 minutes
MAKES:	48 dumplings

2 tbsps salad or olive oil
2 cups lean ground beef or lamb
2 green onions, chopped
2½ tbsps light soy sauce
½ tsp salt
1¾ tbsps rice wine or dry sherry
2 tsps cornstarch mixed with 2 tbsps water
Dumpling wrappers (see recipe)

2 tbsps all-purpose flour mixed to a paste with cold water
Oil for deep frying

Heat the 2 tbsps oil in a pan and fry the ground meat and onion for 2-3 minutes. Add the soy sauce, salt and wine. Cook gently for 2 minutes and then stir in the cornstarch and water mixture. Stir over the heat until the mixture thickens. Put the meat mixture into a dish and leave to cool. Divide into equal portions – about 48. Take a round dumpling wrapper and place a portion of filling in the center. Moisten the edges of the wrapper with a little flour and water paste, gather the edges up and over the filling and pinch together to seal. Shape neatly. Continue to make the remaining dumplings in the same way. Deep-fry the dumplings in moderately hot oil, cooking a few dumplings at a time, until they are golden brown. Drain thoroughly on absorbent paper. Serve with chili sauce dip.

Steamed Barbecued Pork Dumplings

PREPARATION TIME: 20 minutes

MICROWAVE COOKING TIME:
17-18 minutes per batch

SERVES: 4 people

2 tsps oil
10oz ground pork
1 clove garlic, minced
Pinch sugar
2 tbsps soy sauce
2 tbsps cornstarch mixed with 3 tbsps
    stock
½ cup hoisin sauce
30 wonton skins

Combine oil, pork and garlic in a casserole dish. Cover and cook on HIGH 5 minutes, breaking up the pork frequently with a fork as it cooks. Mix the sugar, soy sauce, cornstarch and stock. Add to the pork and cook a further 2-3 minutes until sauce thickens and clears. Stir in the hoisin sauce. Fill the wonton skins and pinch the edges together, but leave some of the filling exposed. Place in one layer in a shallow dish, and barely cover with water. Cover the dish with plastic wrap and cook 2 minutes on HIGH and 8 minutes on LOW/ DEFROST. Serve hot.

Egg Drop Soup

PREPARATION TIME: 10 minutes

COOKING TIME: 8 minutes

SERVES: 6 people

This soup derives its name from stirring beaten eggs into the boiling hot soup. On hitting the soup, the egg cooks and forms threads. The eggs can also be carefully dropped in whole, so that they cook without breaking in the hot soup.

6¼ cups chicken broth
3 green onions, finely chopped
½ cup frozen peas, or shelled fresh peas
1 bunch watercress, finely chopped
A few thin slices of fresh root ginger
Salt and freshly ground black pepper to
    taste

1 tbsp light soy sauce
Pinch of monosodium glutamate
    (optional)
1 tsp cornstarch blended with 1 tbsp water
4 eggs, beaten (or 6-8 whole eggs, see
    below)

Bring the chicken broth to the boil with the green onions, peas, watercress, ginger and salt and pepper to taste. Allow to simmer for 2-3 minutes. Add the soy sauce, monosodium glutamate and the blended cornstarch. Stir well until the soup is transparent and thick. Bring the soup back to the boil and stir in the beaten eggs. Serve immediately. Alternatively, put a whole egg into each warm soup bowl and ladle the hot soup over the top.

Crab Rolls

PREPARATION TIME: 20 minutes

COOKING TIME: 20 minutes

MAKES: 12 rolls

1 cup crab meat, fresh or canned
3 green onions, finely sliced
12 spring roll (egg roll) wrappers
1oz cellophane noodles
¼ tsp grated ginger root
1 tsp oyster sauce
2 tbsps finely chopped bamboo shoots
Salt
Vegetable or peanut oil for deep frying

Soak cellophane noodles in hot water for 8 minutes, or as directed, and drain. Flake crab meat, and drain if necessary. Combine crab meat with green onions, noodles, ginger, bamboo shoots, oyster sauce, and salt to taste. Place spring roll wrappers with one corner pointing towards you. Spoon some of the mixture just before the center. Fold over the corner nearest you and roll to center. Fold the two side points into the center, and roll up completely. They may be sealed with a paste of flour and water if necessary. Refrigerate until needed. Heat oil in wok and deep fry batches of spring rolls just before serving. Drain on paper towels. Serve warm with ginger sauce or sweet-and-sour sauce.

Rice Paper Shrimp Parcels

PREPARATION TIME: 15 minutes

COOKING TIME: 15 minutes

MAKES: about 20 parcels

8oz shrimp, shelled and de-veined
6 green onions, sliced finely
1 packet rice paper
1 egg white
½ tsp cornstarch
⅔ cup peanut oil
1 tsp Chinese wine, or 2 tsps dry sherry
1 tsp light soy sauce
1 tsp sugar
Salt
Pepper

Dry prepared shrimp on paper towels. Mix egg white, cornstarch, wine, sugar, soy sauce, green onions and seasoning together. Mix in shrimp. Heat peanut oil in wok until hot. Wrap five or six shrimp in each piece of rice paper. Gently drop in rice paper parcels and deep fry for about 5 minutes. Serve hot.

Steamed Chicken Wontons

PREPARATION TIME: 20 minutes

MICROWAVE COOKING TIME:
10 minutes per batch

SERVES: 4 people

10oz ground chicken
2 chopped green onions
2 chopped water chestnuts
Small piece ginger root, peeled and grated
2 tbsps light soy sauce
1 tbsp rice wine
1 tbsp sesame oil
1 egg, beaten
Pinch sugar
Salt and pepper
30 fresh wonton skins

Grind raw chicken in a food processor and combine with the remaining ingredients except the

Facing page: Steamed Chicken Wontons (top) and Steamed Barbecued Pork Dumplings (bottom) – served with Sweet and Sour and Hot Mustard Sauces.

wonton skins. Place a teaspoonful of the mixture in the center of each wonton and twist the ends together to seal. Brush lightly with water if the ends won't stick together. Place wontons in one layer in a casserole dish and barely cover with water. Cover with plastic wrap. Cook in 2 batches for 2 minutes on HIGH and 8 minutes on LOW/ DEFROST. Remove with a draining spoon. Serve with Sweet and Sour and Hot Mustard sauces..

Hot and Sour Soup

PREPARATION TIME: 30 minutes
COOKING TIME: 30 minutes
SERVES: 4 people

4oz lean pork fillet
4 dried Chinese mushrooms
⅓ cup bamboo shoots, sliced
1 square beancurd, diced
2 tbsps sunflower or vegetable oil
5 cups light, clear stock, or hot water plus
  2 chicken bouillon cubes
1 tsp cornstarch
2 tbsps cold water
1 tsp sesame oil

MARINADE
1 tbsp light soy sauce
3 tbsps brown vinegar
2 tbsps water
1 tsp sesame oil
Salt
Pepper

GARNISH
Fresh coriander

Soak Chinese mushrooms for 20 minutes in hot water. Meanwhile, slice pork into thin slivers. Make the marinade by combining light soy sauce, brown vinegar, water, sesame oil, and salt and pepper. Pour over pork and leave for 30 minutes. Drain mushrooms. Remove and discard stalks. Slice caps very finely. Remove pork from marinade, and reserve marinade. Heat wok, and add sunflower or vegetable oil. When hot, stir-fry pork, mushrooms and bamboo shoots for 2 minutes. Add stock and bring to the boil. Simmer for 10 minutes. Add beancurd, marinade, and salt and pepper to taste. Slake cornstarch in 2 tbsps of cold water. Add to soup and allow to simmer for 5 minutes. Add sesame oil and sprinkle with fresh coriander. Serve hot.

Chicken and Asparagus Soup

PREPARATION TIME: 10 minutes
COOKING TIME: 45 minutes
SERVES: 4 people

1lb chicken pieces
1 onion, peeled and chopped roughly
1 carrot, chopped roughly
1 stick celery, chopped roughly
4 peppercorns
10oz can asparagus pieces
5 cups water
Salt
Pepper

GARNISH
Chopped parsley

Remove chicken meat from bones and cut into fine shreds. Put chicken bones, onion, carrot, celery, peppercorns and water in wok, and season with salt and pepper. Bring to the boil, reduce heat, and simmer for 30 minutes. Strain and return stock to wok. Add chicken shreds, and simmer until chicken is cooked. Add undrained asparagus pieces. Adjust seasoning. Serve sprinkled with chopped parsley.

Crab and Watercress Soup

PREPARATION TIME: 10 minutes
COOKING TIME: 8-9 minutes
SERVES: 6 people

6¼ cups chicken broth
⅔ cup white crab meat, shredded
2 green onions, finely chopped
2 bunches watercress, finely chopped
Salt and freshly ground black pepper to
  taste
1 tsp cornstarch
1 tbsp water
2 tsps light soy sauce
A few drops sesame oil

Chicken and Asparagus Soup (below) and Hot and Sour Soup (right).

Bring the broth to the boil with the crab meat, onions and watercress and simmer for 4-5 minutes. Add salt and pepper to taste. Mix the cornstarch with the water and add to the soup. Allow to simmer for a further 2 minutes. Add soy sauce and sesame oil, mix well and simmer for 2 minutes. Serve immediately.

Spring Rolls (Egg Rolls)

PREPARATION TIME: 20 minutes

COOKING TIME: 30 minutes

MAKES: 12 rolls

8oz finely ground pork
1 red chili pepper, seeds removed, and
*   sliced finely*
10 canned water chestnuts, chopped
1 onion, peeled and chopped finely
1 clove garlic, crushed
½ tsp grated ginger root
1 tsp ground turmeric
2 tbsps peanut oil
12 spring roll (egg roll) wrappers
Salt
Pepper
Peanut or vegetable oil for deep frying

Heat wok, add 2 tbsps of peanut oil, and fry garlic, ginger, ground turmeric and onion for 3 minutes. Add pork, and stir-fry until pork is browning. Add water chestnuts and chili pepper, and salt and pepper to taste, and fry for a further 2 minutes. Remove from wok, and set aside to cool. Place spring roll wrapper with one corner pointing towards you. Spoon some of the mixture just in front of the center. Fold over the corner nearest to you, and roll to center. Fold the two side points into the center and finish rolling up. They may be sealed with a paste of water and flour if necessary. Refrigerate until needed. Heat oil for deep frying

in wok, and deep fry spring rolls in batches just before needed. Drain on paper towels, and serve warm with chili or sweet-and-sour sauce.

Shrimp and Lettuce Soup

PREPARATION TIME: 10 minutes

MICROWAVE COOKING TIME:
12 minutes plus 5 minutes standing time

SERVES: 4 people

12oz peeled shrimp
1 cup rice
4 cups hot chicken stock
1 piece fresh ginger root, grated
1 small head lettuce, shredded
Salt

Put the rice, stock and ginger into a large, deep bowl. Partially cover and cook 12 minutes on HIGH, stirring often. Cook until the rice softens completely. Add the shrimp, lettuce and salt. Leave the soup to stand, covered, for 5 minutes. Shrimp should heat through in the stock.

Shrimp Toast

PREPARATION TIME: 15 minutes

COOKING TIME: 15 minutes

MAKES: approximately 20 pieces

8oz shrimp, shelled and de-veined, and
*   chopped finely*
1 small egg, beaten
2 tsps sherry
2 tsps oyster sauce
½ tsp grated ginger root
2 tsps cornstarch
Salt
5 slices white bread
Oil for deep frying

Combine shrimp, beaten egg, sherry, oyster sauce, grated ginger, cornstarch and a pinch of salt. Using a 1½" round pastry cutter, cut out circles of bread. Spread mixture on each piece of bread to cover well. Heat oil in wok for deep frying. Fry in batches with bread side up first, until bread is golden brown. Remove and drain on paper towels. Keep hot until all frying is completed.

Crab and Sweet Corn Soup

PREPARATION TIME: 8 minutes

COOKING TIME: 8 minutes

SERVES: 6 people

3 tbsps water or broth
2 tbsps cornstarch
6¼ cups chicken broth
1½ cups canned creamed corn
⅔ cup white crab meat, shredded
Salt and freshly ground black pepper to
*   taste*
1 tsp soy sauce
Pinch monosodium glutamate (optional)

Blend water and cornstarch together. Bring the broth to the boil in a large pan. Add the corn, crab, salt and pepper to taste, soy sauce and monosodium glutamate. Simmer for 4-5 minutes. Add the blended cornstarch to the soup and stir over a gentle heat until the soup thickens. Serve immediately. Whisked egg whites can be stirred into the hot soup just before serving, if liked.

Facing page: Shrimp Toast (top) and Spring Rolls (Egg Rolls) (bottom).

RICE, NOODLES AND EGGS

Rice Noodles Singapore Style

PREPARATION TIME: 15 minutes, plus soaking time for noodles

COOKING TIME: about 15 minutes

SERVES: 4-6 people

8oz rice noodles
Salad or olive oil
2 eggs, beaten
½ inch fresh root ginger, peeled and
    shredded
1½ cups bean sprouts
1 cup cooked ham, pork or chicken,
    shredded
3 tbsps chives, finely chopped
2 cloves garlic, finely chopped
Salt to taste
2 tbsps chicken broth
3 tbsps soy sauce
3 green onions, chopped

Soak the rice noodles in warm water for 10 minutes and then drain well. Heat 1 tbsp oil in a skillet or wok and fry the beaten eggs to make a thin pancake. Slide onto a plate and cut into thin strips. Heat the wok or skillet and add 1 tbsp oil. Fry the ginger and bean sprouts for 2 minutes. Slide onto a plate. Heat the wok or skillet with a further 1 tbsp oil and fry the pork or chicken and the chives for 1-2 minutes. Slide onto a plate. Heat 2 tbsps oil in the wok or skillet and brown the garlic. Add the rice noodles and stir-fry for 2-3 minutes. Add salt to taste, chicken broth, bean sprouts and pork or chicken. Mix well, sprinkle with soy sauce and stir over the heat for 1

minute. Top with the strips of egg pancake and spring onions and serve immediately.

Noodles in Soup

PREPARATION TIME: 10 minutes

COOKING TIME: 6-8 minutes

SERVES: 4-6 people

1lb small rounds of cake noodles
Salt
5½ cups chicken or beef broth
1 cup cooked shredded chicken
2 eggs, hard boiled and sliced
1⅓ cups Chinese napa cabbage, or iceberg
    lettuce, finely shredded
2 green onions, thinly sliced

Cook the noodles in boiling, salted water for 5 minutes. Drain thoroughly. Heat the broth and add salt to taste. Serve the cooked noodles in bowls, and pour over the hot broth. Garnish with chicken, sliced eggs, cabbage and green onions.

Meat and Shrimp Chow Mein

PREPARATION TIME: 20 minutes

COOKING TIME: 12-15 minutes

SERVES: 4-6 people

1lb dried Chinese noodles, or broken
    spaghetti
Salt to taste
4 tbsps salad or olive oil

2-3 green onions, chopped
1 cup cooked ham, shredded
1 cup large shrimp, peeled and de-veined
1 cup shredded carrots
1 cup green beans, sliced
1 tsp fine granulated sugar
1½ tbsps rice wine or dry sherry
1 cup cooked chicken, shredded
1½ cups bean sprouts
3½ tbsps soy sauce

Cook the noodles in boiling, salted water for 4-5 minutes. Rinse under cold water and drain thoroughly. Toss in 1 tbsp oil. Heat the remaining oil in a wok. Add the onions, ham, shrimp, carrots and green beans and stir-fry for 2-3 minutes. Add the salt, sugar, wine, chicken and bean sprouts. Cook for 2 minutes. Add the cooked noodles and soy sauce. Cook for 1-2 minutes. Serve immediately.

Egg Pancakes with Filling

PREPARATION TIME: 10 minutes

COOKING TIME: 6-7 minutes for
                    each pancake

SERVES: 4-6 people

6 eggs
Salt and freshly ground black pepper to
    taste

Facing page: Meat and Shrimp Chow Mein (top), Noodles in Soup (center) and Rice Noodles Singapore Style (bottom).

Ham and Bean Fried Rice

PREPARATION TIME: 15 minutes

MICROWAVE COOKING TIME:
9 minutes plus 2 minutes
standing time

SERVES: 4 people

3 tbsps oil
2 eggs, beaten
Salt and pepper
½ cup ham, chopped
4oz green beans, cut in thin, diagonal
   slices
3 cups cooked rice
1 tbsp soy sauce
4 green onions, chopped

Heat a browning dish 5 minutes on
HIGH. Pour in half the oil and half
the beaten egg and cook for
30 seconds on HIGH on one side.
Turn over and cook for 30 seconds
on the second side. Repeat with
remaining egg. Keep the egg warm
and add the remaining oil to the dish.
Heat for 1 minute on HIGH and add
the ham. Cover the dish and cook
for 1 minute on HIGH. Add the rice
and cook, covered, for 5 minutes on
HIGH. Add the beans, soy sauce and
onions. Cook 1 minute on HIGH and
toss the ingredients to mix well. Slice
the eggs into thin strips and scatter
over the top of the rice. Cover the
dish and leave to stand for 2 minutes
before serving.

Egg Fu Yung

PREPARATION TIME: 5 minutes

COOKING TIME: 8-10 minutes

SERVES: 3-4 people

6 eggs
1½ tbsps soy sauce
3-4 green onions, chopped
Salt and freshly ground black pepper to
   taste
3 tbsps oil
1½ cups bean sprouts

Beat the eggs and soy sauce together
and add the green onions and salt and
pepper to taste. Heat the oil in a skillet

1 cup lean pork, finely chopped or ground
½ cup small cap mushrooms, chopped
1 tsp rice wine or dry sherry
1 tsp light soy sauce
½ tsp fine granulated sugar
1 tsp fresh root ginger, minced
Oil

Beat the eggs and season with salt and
pepper. Mix the pork with the
mushrooms, wine, soy sauce, sugar and
ginger. Add salt and pepper to taste
and mix well. Heat the wok and add 1
tsp oil. Spoon in 3 tbsps of the beaten
egg and spread into a 3 inch circle.
Place 3 tsps filling into the center of the
egg. When the underside of the egg

**This page: Eight Precious Rice (page
42) (top) and Ham and Bean Fried Rice
(bottom). Facing page: Shrimp in Egg
Custard (page 34) (top left), Egg
Pancakes with Filling (page 30) (top
right), Shrimp Fu Yung (page 36)
(center left) and Egg Fu Yung (bottom
right).**

sets but the top is still moist, fold the
egg circle over to make a crescent
shape; press gently to seal the edges.
Cook for 4 minutes on a low heat to
cook the filling. Make the remaining
pancakes in the same way. Serve with a
chili sauce or dip, or with stir-fried
vegetables as a main dish.

or wok and stir-fry the bean sprouts for 2-3 minutes. Pour in the beaten egg mixture. Leave over a moderate heat to set. Broil to set and brown the top. Cut into wedges and serve immediately. Alternatively, stir the mixture while it is cooking so that it turns out like scrambled egg.

Shrimp in Egg Custard

PREPARATION TIME: 5 minutes
COOKING TIME: 20 minutes
SERVES: 6 people

8 eggs
Salt and freshly ground black pepper to taste
Pinch monosodium glutamate (optional)
1 tsp Shao Hsing wine
1¼ cups chicken broth
1¼ cups water
1lb large shrimp, peeled and de-veined
2 tsp cooked oil

Beat the eggs in a bowl, add the seasoning, MSG and wine. Bring the broth and water to the boil and add to the eggs. Add shrimp and set the bowl over a steamer. Cover and steam over simmering water for about 15-20 minutes, until the custard has set. Serve with the cooked oil spooned over the top.

Plain Rice

PREPARATION TIME: 5 minutes
COOKING TIME: 5-7 minutes
SERVES: 4-6 people

1lb rice
Pinch salt
2 tsps salad or olive oil

To make a bowl of plain rice, take any grade of long or medium grain rice. Wash the rice in 4-5 changes of water and then add enough cold water to come 1 inch above the rice level. Add the salt and oil and bring to the boil. Stir once. Cover and simmer gently for 5-7 minutes until the water has been totally absorbed. Remove from the heat and serve. Plain boiled rice should be fluffy, yet have enough moisture around the rice so that the grains can be picked up easily by chopsticks.

Sizzling Rice or Singing Rice

PREPARATION TIME: 50 minutes
COOKING TIME: 2 hours, plus time for deep-frying sizzling rice

4oz short grain rice

When rice is cooked, the crust that forms on the bottom of the pot can be dried and then deep-fried. When it is immersed in gravy or soup it makes a sizzling noise, hence the name. Once made or collected, the rice crusts can be kept for months.

TO MAKE A RICE CRUST
Wash rice in 4-5 changes of water until the water runs clear. Drain the rice and put it into a pan with 1¼ cups of water;

Shrimp Egg Rice (page 36) (below), Sizzling Rice or Singing Rice (bottom left) and Plain Rice (bottom right).

bring to the boil. Reduce heat to low and cook for 20 minutes, simmering gently. Turn off the heat and let the rice stand, covered, for 25-30 minutes. Take a non-stick skillet and transfer the rice to it. Spread evenly to a thickness of ½ inch. Cook on a very gentle heat for 40-50 minutes. Turn over and cook gently for another hour. The rice should be very dry. Break into 2 inch squares and store in a glass jar with a lid.

TO COOK SIZZLING RICE
Pour oil into a pan to a depth of 2 inches and bring to a moderately high temperature (375°F). Add the rice squares and fry until golden brown. Remove and drain on kitchen paper. Serve with soup or any stir-fried dish.

Tossed Noodles

PREPARATION TIME: 20 minutes

MICROWAVE COOKING TIME:
10 minutes plus 5 minutes
standing time

SERVES: 6 people

1lb Chinese egg noodles
4 cups boiling water

½ cup soy sauce mixed with 2 tbsps
  cornstarch
3oz lean steak, cut in short, thin strips
1 tbsp oil
½ cup brown stock
4 green onions, sliced
½ cucumber, sliced
1 small piece white radish, diced
Fresh coriander leaves (Chinese parsley)

Cook noodles as for Velvet Noodles.
Heat a browning dish 5 minutes on
HIGH. Pour in the oil and add the
steak. Cook 2 minutes on HIGH. Stir
in the soy sauce, cornstarch and the
stock. Cover and cook 3 minutes on
HIGH. Add more stock if the sauce
is too thick. Add the onions,
cucumber and radish to the sauce,
and leave to stand 5 minutes before
serving. Pour over noodles and toss
before serving. Garnish with whole
coriander leaves.

Shrimp Egg Rice

PREPARATION TIME: 20 minutes

COOKING TIME: 17-18 minutes

SERVES: 4-6 people

1lb long or medium grain rice
2 eggs
½ tsp salt
4 tbsps oil
2 green onions, chopped
1 large onion, peeled and chopped
2 cloves garlic, peeled and chopped
1 cup small peeled shrimp
½ cup shelled peas, lightly cooked
2 tbsps dark soy sauce

Wash rice in 4-5 changes of water. Add
cold water to come 1 inch above the
rice level and bring to the boil. Stir
once and reduce the heat to simmer.

Cover the pan and gently cook the rice
for 5-7 minutes until the rice is dry and
the liquid has been totally absorbed.
Remove from the heat, add cold water
to cover and drain thoroughly. Spread
the rice on a large tray and separate the
grains with a fork.
Beat the eggs in a bowl and season with
a pinch of salt. Heat the wok and add 1
tbsp oil. Add the onions and stir-fry for
2 minutes. Add the beaten eggs. Allow
to set slightly and then stir the mixture
until it scrambles. Remove onto a plate.
Heat the wok and add 1 tbsp oil. Fry
the garlic for 1 minute then add the
shrimp and cook for 2 minutes. Add
the peas, and stir-fry for 1 minute.
Remove onto a plate. Heat the wok
and add the remaining oil, a little salt to
taste and the cooked rice. Stir-fry to
heat the rice through. Stir in the soy
sauce, shrimp mixture and the cooked
eggs, gently stirring the mixture to
blend. Serve immediately.

Shrimp Fu Yung

PREPARATION TIME: 10 minutes

COOKING TIME: 4 minutes for filling;
3-4 minutes for each pancake

SERVES: 6 people

Salad or olive oil
1-2 cloves of garlic, chopped
1 cup small shrimp, peeled
1 cup green beans, sliced
1 carrot, shredded
6 eggs

SAUCE
Salt and freshly ground black pepper to
  taste
1 cup chicken broth
¼ tsp salt
3 tsps soy sauce
1 tsp fine granulated sugar
1 tsp vinegar
1½ tsps cornstarch

Heat 2 tbsps oil in a wok. Add the
garlic and stir-fry for 1 minute. Add the
shrimp and stir-fry for 1 minute. Add
the beans and carrot and stir-fry for 2
minutes. Remove and keep on one
side. Beat the eggs with salt and pepper
to taste, and add the cooled shrimp
mixture. Clean the wok and heat 1 tsp

oil. Pour in 5 tbsps of the egg mixture
and cook like a pancake. When the egg
is set, turn the pancake over and cook
on the other side until lightly golden.
Place on a warm platter and keep
warm.

TO MAKE THE SAUCE
Beat the broth with the other sauce
ingredients and stir over a gentle heat
until the sauce thickens. Serve the
pancakes with this sauce.

Velvet Noodles

PREPARATION TIME: 20 minutes

MICROWAVE COOKING TIME:
8-12 minutes plus 5 minutes
standing time

SERVES: 6 people

1½ tbsps light soy sauce
1 tbsp cornstarch
Dash sesame oil
3oz lean pork cut in small, thin slices
½ cup mushrooms, sliced
2 cups chicken stock
Salt
4 cups boiling water
2 packages medium Chinese noodles
½ head Chinese cabbage, shredded

Mix soy sauce, cornstarch and
sesame oil together in a large bowl.
Stir in the stock gradually and add
the pork and mushrooms. Cover and
cook for 5-8 minutes on HIGH or
until pork is cooked. Add the
Chinese cabbage and leave to stand,
covered, while cooking the noodles.
Put the noodles and water into a
large, deep bowl. Cook for 3 minutes
on HIGH, stirring occasionally. Leave
to stand 5 minutes before serving.
Add salt to the mushrooms and pork
if desired. Drain the noodles and
arrange on a serving dish. Pour over
the sauce and toss before serving.

**Facing page: Tossed Noodles (top) and
Velvet Noodles (bottom).**

Subgum Fried Rice

PREPARATION TIME: 15 minutes

MICROWAVE COOKING TIME:
7 minutes plus 2 minutes
standing time

SERVES: 4 people

3 tbsps oil
3 cups cooked rice
2 sticks celery, cut into small dice
½ cup mushrooms, roughly chopped
½ red pepper, diced
3 eggs, beaten
1 tbsp light soy sauce
Dash sesame oil
Salt and pepper

GARNISH
2 green onions, sliced diagonally

Heat oil in a large bowl for 1 minute
on HIGH. Add the rice and cook
5 minutes on HIGH, covered. Stir in
the eggs, soy sauce and vegetables
and cook 2 minutes on HIGH. Add
the sesame oil, salt and pepper and
leave to stand 2 minutes before
serving. Garnish with onions.

Fried Rice with Egg

PREPARATION TIME: 15 minutes

MICROWAVE COOKING TIME:
8-10 minutes plus standing time

SERVES: 4 people

3 tbsps oil
2 green onions, finely chopped
3 cups cooked rice
3 eggs, beaten
2 tsps white wine
Salt and pepper
Dash sesame oil

GARNISH
2 green onions, shredded

Put the oil and the finely chopped
onions into a large bowl and heat for
1 minute on HIGH. Add the rice and
cook for 5-7 minutes on HIGH, until

**Fried Rice with Egg (top) and Subgum
Fried Rice (bottom).**

very hot. Stir in the eggs, wine, salt, pepper and sesame oil and cook for 2 minutes on HIGH. Stir carefully and leave to stand, covered, several minutes before serving. Garnish with the shredded onions. Serve with soy sauce, or as an accompaniment to other dishes.

Stir-Fried Eggs with Shredded Meats and Vegetables

PREPARATION TIME: 15-20 minutes

COOKING TIME: 15 minutes

SERVES: 4 people

½ cup cooked chicken, shredded
¾ cup cooked pork or beef, shredded
Salt to taste
¼ tsp soy sauce
4 tbsps salad or olive oil
4 eggs, beaten
2 green onions, chopped
⅓ cup dried mushrooms, soaked and sliced

⅓ button mushrooms, sliced
2 cloud ear fungus, boiled in water for 3 minutes and thinly sliced
2 cups Chinese white cabbage, broccoli or green leafy cabbage, shredded
1-2 green or red chilies, chopped
2 sprigs Chinese parsley, chopped
Pinch monosodium glutamate (optional)

Put the chicken and pork into a bowl with ¼ tsp salt and the soy sauce. Leave for 10 minutes. Heat the wok and add 2 tbsps oil. Add the beaten eggs and stir-fry for 2-3 minutes until they resemble scrambled egg. Keep on one side. Reheat the wok and add the remaining oil. Fry the onions and meats for 2 minutes. Remove from the wok and keep on one side. Stir-fry the cabbage and chilies in the wok for 1-2 minutes. Cover and gently cook in its own juice until tender – approx 3-4 minutes. Return the meats, mushrooms and egg to the cabbage and add the parsley and MSG. Stir-fry for 1-2 minutes. Serve with extra soy sauce and Shao Hsing wine sprinkled over it, if desired.

Above left: Vegetable Rice (top), Assorted Meat Congee (page 42) (center right) and Rice Supreme (page 42) (bottom). **Above:** Noodles with Beef and Almonds (page 43) (top), Egg Noodles with Meat Sauce (page 44) (center) and Fried Noodles with Shredded Chicken (bottom). **Facing page:** Marbled Eggs (page 42) (top), Noodles with Pork Fu Yung (center right) and Stir-Fried Eggs with Shredded Meats and Vegetables (bottom left).

Noodles with Pork Fu Yung

PREPARATION TIME: 20 minutes

COOKING TIME: about 20 minutes

SERVES: 4 people

½ tsp baking soda
1 tbsp water
8oz lean pork, thinly sliced
8oz cake noodles
2 tsps cornstarch
Few drops sesame oil
Salt and freshly ground black pepper to taste

and stir-fry for 1-2 minutes. Add the pork and then pour in the beaten eggs, mixing well. Add the cornstarch, sesame oil and sugar and cook until the mixture thickens. Pour over the noodles and serve immediately.

Vegetable Rice

PREPARATION TIME: 10 minutes	
COOKING TIME: 5-8 minutes	
SERVES: 6-8 people	

1lb rice, cooked
2 cups Chinese cabbage, or Chinese
    leaves, shredded
1 cup sliced green beans
¾ cup frozen peas
3 green onions, chopped
1½ tbsps light soy sauce
Salt to taste

Rinse the cooked rice in cold water and drain. Put the moist rice into a pan. Arrange the Chinese cabbage, sliced beans, peas and onions on top. Cover and cook over a gentle heat for 4-6 minutes. Sprinkle with soy sauce and add salt to taste. Stir the vegetables evenly into the rice and raise the heat for a few seconds. Serve immediately.

Fried Noodles with Shredded Chicken

PREPARATION TIME: 15 minutes	
COOKING TIME: about 10 minutes	
SERVES: 4 people	

Salad or olive oil
2 cups cooked chicken, shredded
1 clove of garlic, chopped
2-3 green onions, chopped
4oz whole green beans (or long Chinese
    beans, cut into 3 inch pieces)
1lb noodles, cooked until just tender
1½ tbsps cornstarch
1 cup chicken broth
2 tbsps soy sauce
2 tbsps oyster sauce
½ tsp wine
½ tsp fine granulated sugar
¼ tsp salt

Heat 2 tbsps oil in a wok and cook the

½ tsp fine granulated sugar
Salad or olive oil
2 cloves of garlic, finely chopped
1 inch fresh root ginger, peeled and sliced
2-3 green onions, chopped
6 eggs, well beaten

Mix the baking soda and the water together. Mix in the pork and marinate for 10-12 minutes. Drain. Cook the noodles in boiling, salted water for 3-4

minutes. Drain, rinse in cold water and drain once again. Toss in 1 tbsp oil. Heat 2 tbsps oil in the wok and brown the garlic. Add 1 tsp salt and the noodles and stir-fry for 3-4 minutes, until they turn light brown. Remove and keep on one side. Heat sufficient oil for deep-frying in the wok and deep-fry the pork for 3-4 minutes, drain and remove. Tip off the oil. Heat 1 tbsp oil in the wok. Add the ginger and onions chicken for 2 minutes. Remove the chicken. Add the garlic, green onions and beans and fry for 2 minutes. Remove the vegetables. Heat 2 tbsps oil in the wok and toss the pre-boiled noodles over the heat for 2 minutes. Arrange on a plate and keep warm. Return the fried chicken, onion and green beans to the wok and stir-fry for 1 minute. Dissolve the cornstarch in the chicken broth and add to the wok. Add the soy sauce, oyster sauce, wine, sugar and salt and pepper to taste. Simmer until the sauce is thick. Pour over the bed of noodles and serve immediately.

Marbled Eggs

PREPARATION TIME: 10 minutes

COOKING TIME: 1 hour
10 minutes to 1 hour 15 minutes

MAKES: 6-8

These are eaten cold, dipped in a sauce, as a starter or a snack. Allow 1 egg per person.

6-8 eggs
4 tbsps tea leaves
1 inch cinnamon stick
2-3 star anise
3 tbsps dark soy sauce
2 tbsps light soy sauce

Boil the eggs for 8-10 minutes until hard boiled. Drain and cool quickly by placing in iced water. Tap each egg shell with the back of a spoon until cracks appear all over. Bring enough water to the boil to cover the eggs. Add tea leaves, cinnamon, star anise, soy sauces and stir. Add the eggs and simmer gently for at least 1 hour. Allow to cool and then shell before serving.

Eight Precious Rice

PREPARATION TIME: 20 minutes

MICROWAVE COOKING TIME:
10 minutes plus 2 minutes
standing time

SERVES: 4 people

3 tbsps oil
4oz chicken, cut in ½ inch cubes
4oz frozen peas

2oz shrimp
¼ cup diced bamboo shoots
8 water chestnuts, sliced thinly
½ cup mushrooms, sliced thinly
4 green onions, chopped
3 cups cooked rice
2 eggs, beaten
2 tbsps soy sauce
Salt and pepper

Heat oil in a large bowl 1 minute on HIGH. Add the chicken and cook, stirring frequently, for 3 minutes on HIGH. Cover the bowl loosely. Add the rice and cook 5 minutes on HIGH to heat through. Add the remaining ingredients and cook 1 minute on HIGH. Leave to stand, covered, 2 minutes before serving.

Deep-Fried Noodles

Boil noodles for 5 minutes. Drain thoroughly on absorbent paper. Deep-fry in hot oil until crisp and golden.

Fried Rice Noodles

PREPARATION TIME: 25 minutes

COOKING TIME: 10 minutes

SERVES: 4-6 people

1lb rice noodles
3 tbsps salad or olive oil
1 cup cooked chicken, shredded
½ cup small shrimp, peeled and de-veined
½ cup bamboo shoots, sliced
2 sticks celery, chopped
1 leek, chopped
2 green onions, shredded
4 tbsps broth
3 tbsps soy sauce

Soak the rice noodles in warm water for 10-15 minutes. Drain thoroughly. Heat half the oil in a wok. Add the chicken, shrimp, bamboo shoots, celery, leeks and green onions and stir-fry for 2-3 minutes. Add the broth and salt and pepper to taste. Simmer for 2 minutes and then drain the chicken and vegetables. Heat the remaining oil, add the rice noodles and stir over the heat for 1 minute. Add the soy sauce and stir into the chicken and vegetable mixture. Cook together for 2-3 minutes. Serve immediately.

Assorted Meat Congee

PREPARATION TIME: 20 minutes

COOKING TIME: 1 hour 45 minutes

SERVES: 6 people

1lb rice
9½ cups chicken broth
4oz tripe, well washed and chopped (optional)
4oz pig's or lamb's liver, sliced
1 cup cooked beef, ham, lamb, chicken or pork, chopped
4oz whitefish fillets, thinly sliced
1 tsp sesame oil
3 green onions, chopped
1½ tsps salt, or to taste
1½ tsps freshly ground black pepper
½ inch fresh root ginger, peeled and sliced

Wash the rice well and put it into a large saucepan. Add the chicken broth and the tripe (if used). Cook gently for 1-1½ hours, or until the tripe is well cooked and the rice has become a soft pulp. In a separate saucepan, boil the sliced liver for 5 minutes in water. Drain and add to the rice. Add the cooked meat, fish, sesame oil, half the onions, salt and pepper and the slices of ginger. Cook for further 10-15 minutes covered. Pour into large bowls and serve topped with the remaining chopped onions.

Rice Supreme

PREPARATION TIME: 10 minutes

COOKING TIME: 15 minutes

SERVES: 6 people

3 tbsps salad or olive oil
1½ tbsps light soy sauce
2 eggs, beaten
1 small onion, peeled and finely sliced
½ cup small shrimp, peeled
½ cup large shrimp, peeled
½ cup whitefish, cubed
2 green onions, finely chopped
½ a small green pepper, seeded and cut into strips
1lb rice, cooked and cooled
Salt to taste
1 tsp freshly ground black pepper
3 tbsps ketchup
½ cup frozen peas

1 inch fresh root ginger, peeled and sliced
8oz lean beef, thinly sliced
½ cup carrots, diced
½ cup sliced green beans
½ cup water chestnuts, sliced
½ cup mushrooms, sliced
2 green chilies, sliced in half
Salt
1 tsp fine granulated sugar
1 tsp monosodium glutamate (optional)
1 cup chicken broth
⅔ cup blanched almonds
1lb noodles, cooked until just tender

Heat 2 tbsps oil in a wok. Fry the onion, garlic, ginger and beef for 3 minutes. Add the carrots and green beans and fry for 2 minutes. Add the water chestnuts, mushrooms and green chilies and fry for 1 minute. Add salt, sugar, MSG and broth. Simmer for 1 minute. Remove to a dish and keep warm. Clean the wok and add the remaining oil. Fry the almonds and noodles for 1-2 minutes. Mix with the cooked vegetables and season with soy sauce. Serve immediately.

Plain Fried Rice

PREPARATION TIME: 5 minutes, plus cooling time

COOKING TIME: 10-11 minutes

SERVES: 4-6 people

1lb Patna or long grain rice
¼ tsp monosodium glutamate
2 tbsps salad or olive oil
Salt

Wash the rice in 4-5 changes of cold water. Drain the rice and put into a large pan or wok. Add sufficient cold water to come 1 inch above the level of the rice. Bring to the boil. Stir once and reduce the heat to simmer. Cover and cook gently for 5-7 minutes until the water has been totally absorbed and the rice is separate and fluffy, with the necessary amount of stickiness to be handled by chopsticks. (If necessary cook for a little longer.) Spread the rice out on a tray and cool. Sprinkle with the monosodium glutamate. Heat the oil in a wok or large skillet and add the rice. Stir-fry for 1-2 minutes. Add salt to taste and stir-fry for a further 1-2 minutes.

Heat 1 tbsp oil in the wok and pour in the beaten eggs. Cook to make a thin omelette. Cut into thin strips. Heat 1 tbsp oil in the wok and stir-fry the onion for 2 minutes. Add the shrimp and fish and stir-fry for 3-4 minutes. Remove the fish mixture to a plate. Heat the remaining oil in the wok. Add half the green onions and the green pepper and stir-fry for 2 minutes. Add the rice and season with salt and pepper. Add the ketchup, peas, fried fish and shrimp. Add the soy sauce and stir-fry for 3 minutes. Serve with the egg strips arranged on top of the rice. Sprinkle with the remaining chopped green onions.

Above: Deep-Fried Noodles (top), Stir-Fried Shanghai Noodles (page 44) (center) and Fried Rice Noodles (bottom).

Noodles with Beef and Almonds

PREPARATION TIME: 15 minutes

COOKING TIME: 10 minutes

SERVES: 4 people

3 tbsps salad or olive oil
1 onion, chopped
4 cloves of garlic, chopped

Stir-Fried Shanghai Noodles

PREPARATION TIME: 10 minutes

COOKING TIME: 5-6 minutes

SERVES: 4 people

1½ cups white cabbage, shredded
½ tsp sesame oil
3 tbsps cooked oil
1 cup cooked chicken or pork, shredded
1lb thick Shanghai noodles, cooked until just tender
2½ tbsps soy sauce
½ tsp monosodium glutamate (optional)
Freshly ground black pepper to taste

Cook the cabbage in boiling water for 1 minute. Drain thoroughly. Heat the oils in a wok. Add the meat and stir-fry for 2-3 minutes. Add the cooked noodles, soy sauce, monosodium glutamate and salt and pepper to taste. Add the cabbage, heat through and serve immediately.

Egg Noodles with Meat Sauce

PREPARATION TIME: 15 minutes

COOKING TIME: 20-22 minutes

SERVES: 4-6 people

3 tbsps salad or olive oil
3 cloves garlic, chopped
1 inch fresh root ginger, peeled and shredded
1 onion, chopped
1 green pepper, seeded and sliced
1lb ground beef
½ tsp salt
1 tbsp ketchup
1 tbsp soy sauce
½ tsp freshly ground black pepper
½ cup chicken broth
1 tsp cornstarch
1lb egg noodles
2 green onions, chopped

Heat 2 tbsps oil in a wok. Fry the garlic and ginger for 1-2 minutes. Add the onion and fry for 2-3 minutes. Add the green pepper and the ground beef and fry for 1 minute. Add half the salt, ketchup, soy sauce and ground pepper. Fry for a further 3 minutes. Blend the

broth and cornstarch and add to the wok. Cook until thickened and the meat is tender. Meanwhile, cook noodles in boiling, salted water for 3-4 minutes, and drain. Rinse in cold water and drain once again. Heat the remaining oil in a pan. Add the noodles and toss over the heat until heated through. Arrange on a plate and top with the meat sauce. Garnish with chopped green onions.

Shanghai Noodle Snack

PREPARATION TIME: 15 minutes

MICROWAVE COOKING TIME:
5-6 minutes plus 5 minutes standing time

SERVES: 6 people

1lb Chinese egg noodles
4 cups boiling water

SAUCE
2 tbsps cornstarch dissolved in ¼ cup water
2 tbsps rice wine
1 tbsp light soy sauce
1 cup light stock
1 small piece ginger root, thinly sliced
4 green onions, thinly sliced diagonally
Meat from one large crab or 1 6oz package frozen or canned crabmeat

Cook the noodles in the boiling water for 3 minutes on HIGH. Leave to stand 5 minutes, covered, while preparing the sauce. Combine the first 5 ingredients in a deep bowl, stirring well to mix the cornstarch. Cook 2-3 minutes until the sauce thickens and clears. Add the crab and onion and cook 30 seconds on HIGH. Drain the noodles well and toss with the sauce to serve.

Rice with Ground Beef

PREPARATION TIME: 10 minutes

COOKING TIME: 25 minutes

SERVES: 6 people

2 tbsps salad or olive oil
8oz ground beef

3 green onions, chopped
½ inch fresh root ginger, peeled and sliced
2 cloves garlic, peeled and sliced
1½ tbsps soy sauce
1 green pepper, seeded and chopped
1lb rice, thoroughly washed
½ tsp salt
1 tsp freshly ground black pepper, or to taste

Heat the oil and fry the ground beef, onions, ginger and garlic for 5 minutes. Add the soy sauce and green pepper and fry for 5-6 minutes. Cook the rice with sufficient water to come 1 inch above the rice level, and the salt, for 5-6 minutes or until the rice is semi-cooked, and the water is almost absorbed. Spread the beef evenly over the rice. Cover and cook for 6-8 minutes over a very gentle heat. Remove and serve well mixed. Season with salt and pepper to taste.

Dumpling Wrappers (Chiao Tze P'i)

PREPARATION TIME: 50-60 minutes

MAKES: 40-50 wrappers

2¼ cups all-purpose flour
¾ cup cold water

Sift the flour into a bowl and add the cold water, a little at a time, and mix to a firm dough. Knead the dough on a flat surface for 4-5 minutes. Cover with a damp cloth or wrap in plastic wrap. Leave to stand at room temperature for 30-40 minutes. Roll out on a well-floured surface as thinly as possible, until almost transparent. Cut into round or square pieces to suit your requirements. Use within a few hours of making otherwise they will dry out.

Facing page: Shanghai Noodle Snack.

FISH AND SEAFOOD

Sweet and Sour Fish

PREPARATION TIME: 15 minutes

MICROWAVE COOKING TIME:
11-13 minutes

SERVES: 4 people

4 trout, cleaned and trimmed
2 tbsps sherry
1 small piece ginger root, peeled and sliced
½ cup brown sugar
2 tbsps cornstarch
3 fl oz vinegar
2 tbsps light soy sauce
2 carrots, thinly sliced
1 clove garlic, minced
2 green onions, sliced
Salt and pepper

Place the trout in a shallow dish with the sherry, ginger and enough water to just cover the fish. Cover the dish with pierced plastic wrap and cook 8-9 minutes on HIGH. Remove the fish to a serving dish and peel off the skin from one side. Cover and keep warm. Reserve the cooking liquid from the fish. Combine the remaining ingredients except the green onions and carrots in a deep bowl. Cook for 2-3 minutes on HIGH or until the sauce thickens and clears. Thin down the sauce with some of the fish cooking liquid until of thick coating consistency. Add the carrots and onions and cook 1 minute on HIGH. Pour over some of the sauce to serve with the fish and serve the rest of the sauce separately.

Singapore Fried Noodles

PREPARATION TIME: 20 minutes

COOKING TIME: 25 minutes

This page: Sweet and Sour Fish. Facing page: Singapore Fried Noodles (top) and Steamed Fish with Black Beans (page 48) (bottom).

SERVES: 4 people

8oz packet egg noodles
8oz shrimp, shelled and de-veined
1 chicken breast, cut into shreds
1½ cups bean sprouts
2 cloves garlic, crushed
3 sticks celery, sliced diagonally
2 green onions, sliced
1 red chili pepper, seeds removed, and sliced

1 green chili pepper, seeds removed, and sliced
1 tsp chili powder
2 eggs, lightly beaten

3 tbsps oil
Salt
Pepper

GARNISH
Chili flowers (carefully cut end of chili pepper into shreds, and soak in cold water until flower opens)

Soak noodles in boiling water for 8 minutes, or as directed. Drain noodles on paper towels and leave to dry. Heat wok, and add 1 tbsp of oil. Add lightly beaten eggs, and salt and pepper to taste. Stir gently and cook until set. Remove from wok, and cut into thin strips and keep warm. Add remaining oil to wok. When hot, add garlic and chili powder and fry for 30 seconds. Add chicken, celery, green onions and red and green chili peppers, and stir-fry for 8 minutes or until chicken has cooked through. Add noodles, shrimp and bean sprouts, and toss until well mixed and heated through. Serve with scrambled egg strips on top and garnish with chili flowers.

Shrimp with Broccoli

PREPARATION TIME: 10 minutes
COOKING TIME: 8-10 minutes
SERVES: 4 people

1lb peeled medium size shrimp
Oil for deep frying

SAUCE
½ cup chicken broth
2 tsps cornstarch
Freshly ground black pepper and salt to taste
Pinch monosodium glutamate (optional)
1 tsp fine granulated sugar

SEASONING
2 tbsps cooked oil, or oil from deep-frying the shrimps
Pinch salt
½ tsp fine granulated sugar
Pinch monosodium glutamate (optional)
2 tsps cornstarch

8oz Chinese broccoli, or Continental broccoli, cut into 3 inch pieces
1 carrot, peeled and sliced
2 cloves garlic, peeled and chopped
½ inch fresh root ginger, peeled and chopped

Deep-fry the shrimp in hot oil for 1-2 minutes. Drain the shrimp and keep on one side. Keep the oil. Mix the sauce ingredients together. Mix the seasoning ingredients together in a separate bowl. Cook the broccoli in boiling water for 1 minute. Drain and add cold water to cover. Drain once again and mix the broccoli with the seasoning ingredients. Heat the wok and add 2 tbsps cooked oil. Add the carrot, garlic and ginger and stir-fry for 1 minute. Add the broccoli and stir-fry for 1 minute more. Add the shrimp and stir fry for ½ minute then add the blended sauce ingredients. Cook gently until the sauce thickens. Serve immediately.

Shrimp in Hot Sauce

PREPARATION TIME: 10 minutes
COOKING TIME: 6 minutes
SERVES: 4 people

12oz cooked unshelled shrimp

SEASONING
1 tsp brown vinegar
1 tsp Shao Hsing wine
Pinch salt

SAUCE
1 tsp cornstarch mixed with 1 tbsp water
2 tsps ketchup
Salt and freshly ground black pepper to taste
2 tsps fine granulated sugar
½ tsp monosodium glutamate (optional)
1 tsp hot chili sauce
1 cup chicken broth
2 tbsps cooked oil

Wash shrimp and drain well. Mix the seasoning ingredients together. Mix the sauce ingredients together in a separate bowl. Heat the oil in a wok and deep-fry the shrimp for 1 minute. Remove the shrimp and drain. Keep the oil. Reheat the wok and add 2 tsps oil and stir-fry the onion, celery and garlic for 1 minute. Add shrimp and the blended sauce ingredients. Bring to the boil and simmer gently for 3-4 minutes. Stir in the seasoning mixture.

Steamed Fish with Black Beans

PREPARATION TIME: 15 minutes
COOKING TIME: 15 minutes
SERVES: 4 people

2lbs whole snapper, or bass, cleaned and scaled
1 tbsp salted black beans
2 cloves garlic, crushed
1 tbsp light soy sauce
1 tsp Chinese wine, or 2 tsps dry sherry

Shrimp in Hot Sauce (right), Shrimp with Bean Curd (page 52) (center right) and Shrimp with Broccoli (bottom).

1 tsp sugar
½ tsp cornstarch
1 tsp sesame oil
½ can bamboo shoots, cut into shreds
Salt
Pepper

Wash and clean fish well and dry with paper towels. Make 3 or 4 diagonal cuts in flesh of fish on each side. Rub garlic into cuts and place fish on a heat-proof dish. Rinse black beans in cold water, then crush with the back of a spoon. Add cornstarch, sesame oil, soy sauce, sugar and wine,

This page: Sesame Crab in Asparagus Ring. Facing page: Seafood Combination.

and salt and pepper and mix together well. Pour over fish. Sprinkle bamboo shoots on top of fish. Put plate on top of a bamboo steamer or metal trivet standing in wok. Add water, ensuring the level is below the level of the plate. Cover and bring to the boil. Steam for about 10 minutes after boiling point is reached. Ensure

that the fish is cooked, but do not oversteam. Serve hot.

Seafood Combination

PREPARATION TIME:	20 minutes
COOKING TIME:	20 minutes
SERVES:	4 people

8oz shrimp, shelled and de-veined
4oz squid, cleaned, cut into 1″ rings, opened up, and scored with lattice design

Add shrimp and fish, and toss well. Drain shrimp and fish, reserving sauce. Blanch pea pods in boiling water for 1 minute. Drain. Heat oil in wok. Deep fry shrimp, fish and squid for 2 minutes. Remove from pan and drain on paper towels. Carefully remove oil from wok, reserving 1 tbsp of oil in wok. Heat oil. Stir-fry carrot and celery for 3 minutes. Add pea pods and stir-fry a further 3 minutes. Add any remaining sauce and stir. Add seafood and toss well until heated through.

Sesame Crab in Asparagus Ring

PREPARATION TIME: 20 minutes

MICROWAVE COOKING TIME: 9-10 minutes

SERVES: 4 people

3 tbsps sesame paste (tahini)
2 tbsps light soy sauce
½ cup light stock
2 tbsps sherry
1 tbsp cornstarch
2 tbsps Szechwan peppercorns
2 tbsps oil
1lb asparagus, fresh or frozen, cut on the
    diagonal into 2 inch pieces
2 tbsps Chinese parsley leaves, left whole
4 green onions, thinly sliced or shredded
Salt
Pinch sugar (optional)
1lb crabmeat (including some pink claw
    meat)
Sesame seeds

Combine the first 6 ingredients in a deep bowl. Cook for 2-3 minutes on HIGH, until thick, and set aside. Heat a browning dish 5 minutes on HIGH. Pour in the oil and add the asparagus. Stir-fry on HIGH for 4 minutes. If further cooking is needed, cover the dish and cook 1 minute on HIGH. Add the Chinese parsley, green onions and crabmeat to the reserved sauce. Reheat 1 minute on HIGH. Add salt and sugar if desired. Arrange the asparagus pieces in a ring on a serving dish and pile the crabmeat mixture into the center. Sprinkle with sesame seeds to serve.

4oz pea pods, trimmed
4oz white fish fillets, cut into 1″ cubes
1 stick celery, sliced diagonally
1 carrot, scraped and cut into matchstick
    strips
1 tsp grated ginger root
½ tsp salt

1 tbsp dry white wine
1 egg white
1 tsp cornstarch
Oil for deep frying

Combine wine, salt, egg white, grated ginger and cornstarch and mix well.

Sweet and Sour Shrimp

PREPARATION TIME: 20 minutes

MICROWAVE COOKING TIME:
4-5 minutes plus 2 minutes
standing time

SERVES: 4 people

SAUCE
Double recipe Sweet and Sour Sauce.
Use reserved pineapple juice made up to
2 cups with more canned juice.

1 large green pepper, cut in 1 inch pieces
4 tomatoes, peeled and quartered
4 green onions, cut in 1 inch pieces
8oz can pineapple pieces, juice reserved
1½ lbs shelled shrimp, de-veined

Prepare the Sweet and Sour Sauce.
Add the green pepper to the hot
sauce and cook 1 minute on HIGH.
Add the pineapple, tomatoes, onions,
shrimp and cover tightly. Leave to
stand 3 minutes before serving. Serve
with rice.

Shrimp with Bean Curd

PREPARATION TIME: 10 minutes

COOKING TIME: 8 minutes

SERVES: 4 people

1lb peeled medium size shrimp

SEASONING
1 tsp light soy sauce
Pinch salt
1 tsp fine granulated sugar
1 tsp cornstarch

1 inch fresh root ginger, peeled and finely
chopped
2 tbsps salad or olive oil
1 clove of garlic, peeled and chopped
1 red chili, chopped
2-3 bean curd cakes, cubed
4 tbsps chicken broth
1 tsp cornstarch
2 tbsps water

Mix the shrimp with the seasoning
ingredients and half of the ginger. Heat
the oil and stir-fry the ginger and
shrimp for 2 minutes. Add the garlic

This page: **Kung Pao Shrimp** (top) and
Crabmeat Egg Fu Yung, Cantonese
(page 56) (bottom). Facingg page: **Sweet**
and Sour Shrimp (top) and **Scallops in**
Pepper Sauce (page 56) (bottom).

and fry for 1 minute. Add the chili,
cubed bean curd and broth. Simmer
for 2-3 minutes. Mix the cornstarch
with the water and remaining crushed
ginger and pour over the shrimp
mixture. Simmer gently until the sauce
thickens. Serve immediately.

Kung Pao Shrimp

PREPARATION TIME: 20 minutes

MICROWAVE COOKING TIME:
5 minutes plus 2 minutes
standing time

SERVES: 4 people

1lb shelled jumbo shrimp, de-veined
1 tsp chopped fresh ginger root
1 tsp chopped garlic
Salt and pepper
¼ tsp sugar
1 small onion, coarsely chopped
1 zucchini cut into ½ inch cubes
½ cup roasted cashew nuts

SAUCE

1 tbsp cornstarch
½ cup stock
4 tbsps soy sauce
1 tsp red bean paste (optional)
1 tsp sesame oil
1 tbsp shao-hsing wine or rice wine

Combine the shrimp, ginger, garlic, sugar, salt and pepper in a casserole dish. Cover and refrigerate for 20 minutes. Combine all the sauce ingredients and pour over the shrimp. Cover and cook for 3 minutes on MEDIUM. Stir often and do not allow the shrimp to overcook. Add the remaining ingredients and cook 2 minutes on HIGH. Leave to stand 2 minutes before serving. Serve with rice.

Fish Steamed on Lotus Leaves

PREPARATION TIME: 25 minutes

MICROWAVE COOKING TIME: 13-16 minutes

SERVES: 4 people

4 small fish such as red mullet or small
*   trout*
4 dried Chinese mushrooms, soaked
*   30 minutes in hot water*
3 tbsps shrimp
2 tbsps oil
4 strips bacon, diced
1 small piece fresh ginger root, slivered
4 green onions, finely chopped
2 tbsps soy sauce
1 cup stock
2 tbsps cornstarch, dissolved in 4 tbsps of
*   the mushroom liquid*
Salt and pepper
Sliced lotus root or bamboo shoots, cut in
*   thin strips*
2-4 lotus leaves, depending on size

Trim off the fins of the fish and trim the tails neatly. Set fish aside in the refrigerator until ready to cook. Heat a browning dish for 5 minutes on HIGH. Pour in the oil and add the bacon. Cook 1 minute until beginning to brown. Drain the mushrooms and the shrimp. Dice the mushrooms and add to the bacon along with the shrimp, onions and ginger. Cook a further 1 minute on HIGH or until

bacon is crisp. Place 1 or 2 lotus leaves in the bottom of a large, shallow dish. Lay the fish on top and scatter over the bacon mixture. Cover the fish with the remaining lotus leaves and pour over the soy sauce and stock. Cover the dish and cook the fish on HIGH for 9-11 minutes. When the fish are cooked, remove them and the lotus leaves from the dish and keep them warm. Add the cornstarch to the fish cooking liquid and stir well. Add salt and pepper and cook for 2-3 minutes on HIGH, or until the sauce has thickened. Add the lotus root or bamboo shoots. Remove the top layer of lotus leaves and serve the fish on the bottom leaves with the sauce.

Fish in Wine Sauce

PREPARATION TIME: 20 minutes

COOKING TIME: 15 minutes

SERVES: 3-4 people

MARINADE
¼ tsp salt
1 egg white
2 tsps cornstarch
1 tsp wine-flavored vinegar

10-12oz mullet or carp fillet, cut into 2
*   inch slices*
Oil for deep frying
1 cup chicken broth

SEASONING
Pinch monosodium glutamate (optional)
Pinch salt
Pinch freshly ground black pepper
1 tsp fine granulated sugar
2½ tsps cornstarch
1½ tbsps water
1 cloud ear fungus, soaked and boiled for
*   2 minutes, and then chopped*
2 dried Chinese mushrooms, soaked and
*   sliced*

Mix the marinade ingredients together. Marinate the fish in the marinade for 10 minutes. Heat a generous quantity of oil in the wok and deep-fry the drained fish pieces, a few at a time, until the flesh is white. Remove and drain the fish. Keep the oil for future

use. Clean the wok. Add the chicken stock to the wok and bring to the boil. Simmer gently and stir in the seasoning ingredients. Simmer for few seconds and then add the cornstarch blended with the water. Add the fish and simmer until the sauce thickens. Add the fungus and mushrooms. Simmer for 1 minute. Serve immediately.

Fish with Vegetables and Bean Curd

PREPARATION TIME: 20 minutes

COOKING TIME: 15 minutes

SERVES: 4 people

4 squares bean curd, cut into 1 inch
*   squares*

SAUCE B
1 tbsp Shao Hsing wine
1¼ tbsps dark soy sauce
1¼ tbsps light soy sauce
2½ tsps brown sugar
Pinch salt
Pinch white pepper
3¾ cups chicken broth

8oz cod fillet, cut into 2 inch slices

SEASONING FOR FISH A
½ tsp salt
½ tsp Shao Hsing wine
1¾ tbsps cornstarch

3 tbsps salad or olive oil
1½ cups shredded Chinese cabbage, or
*   Chinese leaves*

SEASONING FOR CABBAGE C
½ tsp brown sugar
Pinch salt
1 tsp cornstarch

1 inch fresh root ginger, peeled and
*   shredded*
2 green onions, chopped
1½ tbsps cornstarch mixed with 2 tbsps
*   water*
½ cup bean sprouts
Few slices of green pepper, diced
1 small carrot, chopped
2 tbsps frozen peas (or lightly cooked fresh
*   ones)*

Soak the bean curd in cold water for

**Above: Fish Steamed on Lotus Leaves.
Above right: Fish with Vegetables and
Bean Curd (top), Fish in Wine Sauce
(center right) and Fish with Chicken
and Vegetables (bottom).**

2 minutes. Drain well. Mix the sauce B
ingredients and keep on one side.
Wash the fish and drain well. Mix
seasoning A ingredients and marinate
fish for 10-12 minutes. Heat the wok
and add half the oil. When very hot,
add the cabbage and seasoning C
ingredients and stir-fry for about
2 minutes. Drain the cabbage well.
Discard any liquid. Heat wok and add
the remaining oil. Add the ginger and
onions and stir-fry for 1 minute. Add
sauce B ingredients and bring to the
boil. Add fish and boil for 1 minute.
Add the bean curd and simmer over a
low heat for 5-6 minutes. (The bean
curd should become spongy to the
touch.) Add the blended cornstarch

and water. Stir and simmer until the
sauce thickens. Add the cabbage and
other vegetables and simmer for a
further 2 minutes. Serve immediately.

Fish with Chicken and Vegetables

PREPARATION TIME: 25 minutes

COOKING TIME: 15 minutes

SERVES: 4 people

1lb plaice or lemon sole fillets, cut into 2
    inch pieces
8oz boned chicken, cut into 2 inch slices
6 dried Chinese mushrooms, soaked and
    sliced
½ cup button mushrooms, sliced
½ cup bamboo shoots, sliced
½ cup shredded mustard green, kale or
    broccoli, or 4 asparagus tips, chopped
1 cup mixed diced vegetables (peas,
    carrots, bean sprouts, etc)

1 small onion, peeled and sliced
1 tsp salt
Cooked oil

MARINADE
¼ tsp salt
1 tsp white pepper
½ tsp monosodium glutamate (optional)
2 tsps cornstarch
1 tbsp cooked oil
¼ tsp sesame oil

SAUCE
1 cup chicken broth
Salt to taste
Freshly ground black pepper to taste
½ tsp monosodium glutamate (optional)
2 tsps cooked oil
1 tsp lemon juice

Wash the fish and drain. Mix the
marinade ingredients together and
marinate fish for 10-15 minutes. Blanch
the mustard green, kale or broccoli in
boiling, salted water for 1 minute. Drain

and keep on one side. Heat the wok with 1 tbsp cooked oil and stir-fry the mixed vegetables and the onions for 2 minutes. Add the mustard green and stir-fry for 1 minute. Drain and remove onto a plate. Brush a deep plate with cooked oil and arrange the drained fish, mushrooms, chicken and bamboo shoots in alternate rows. Place the dish over a steamer. Cover and steam over boiling water for 7 minutes until cooked. Remove the steamer from heat and keep on one side. Heat the wok and add the sauce ingredients and fish marinade. Bring to the boil and simmer for 1 minute, until thickened. Put the steamed fish, mushrooms etc. onto a serving plate and pour the hot sauce over the top. Serve immediately.

Cantonese Lobster

PREPARATION TIME: 30 minutes

MICROWAVE COOKING TIME:
5-6 minutes plus 1 minute standing time

SERVES: 4 people

1 1¼-1½ lb cooked lobster
2 tsps black beans soaked in 2 tbsps water
4-6 dried Chinese mushrooms, soaked 30 minutes in hot water
2 tsps soy sauce
½ cup plus 2 tbsps light stock
4 tbsps rice wine
1 clove garlic, minced
1½ tbsps cornstarch dissolved in 4 tbsps mushroom soaking liquid
3 tbsps chives
1oz pea pods
4 leaves Chinese cabbage, cut into 1 inch strips
1½ oz bean sprouts
5 water chestnuts, sliced
Salt and pepper

Combine the soy sauce, stock, wine and cornstarch. Cook in a deep bowl for 2-3 minutes on HIGH, or until the sauce thickens. If it is too thick, add more of the mushroom soaking liquid. Drain and slice the Chinese mushrooms and add to the sauce with the black beans, slightly crushed. Remove the tail and claw meat from the lobster and as much of the leg meat as possible. Cut the

meat into ½ inch pieces, leaving the claws whole if desired. Add the vegetables to the sauce and cook 2 minutes on HIGH. Stir in the lobster and leave covered for 1 minute before serving. Use the whole claws without their shells as garnish if desired.

Scallops in Pepper Sauce

PREPARATION TIME: 20 minutes

MICROWAVE COOKING TIME:
13-15 minutes

SERVES: 4 people

1lb scallops, shelled and cleaned, roe attached if possible
½ clove garlic, finely chopped
3 tbsps rice wine
3 tbsps light soy sauce
1 tbsp cornstarch dissolved in ⅓ cup light stock
4 tbsps sweet chili sauce
1 small piece fresh ginger root, peeled and chopped
1 green pepper, thinly sliced
4 green onions, sliced or shredded
Pinch sugar
Salt and pepper

If the scallops are large, cut in half, horizontally. Place in a casserole dish with the garlic, wine, soy sauce, sugar and salt and pepper. Cover the dish and cook for 10 minutes on MEDIUM. Remove the scallops and keep warm. Add the cornstarch and stock to the hot cooking liquid and stir well. Add the chili sauce and ginger root and cook 2-3 minutes, or until thickened. Add the green pepper and onions to the sauce and return the scallops to the dish. Cook 1-2 minutes on HIGH, until the scallops are cooked and the vegetables are still crisp. Serve with rice.

Crabmeat Egg Foo Yung, Cantonese

PREPARATION TIME: 20 minutes

MICROWAVE COOKING TIME:
10-13 minutes

SERVES: 4 people

6 eggs
1 cup crabmeat
2 sticks celery, thinly sliced
6 large mushrooms, thinly sliced
1 cup bean sprouts
½ onion, thinly sliced
1 tsp sherry
Salt and pepper
2 tbsps oil

SAUCE
1 tbsp cornstarch
1 tsp sugar
1 cup chicken stock
2 tsp soy sauce
1 tsp sherry
1 tsp sesame oil
½ tsp ketchup
Salt

Heat a browning dish 5 minutes on HIGH. Beat the eggs and mix in the remaining ingredients except the oil and those for the sauce. Add oil to the browning dish and spoon in 2 heaped tbsps of the egg mixture at a time. Cook 2-4 patties at a time for 2-3 minutes on MEDIUM on the first side, turn over and cook 1-2 minutes on the other. Re-heat browning dish after each batch. Keep warm while making the sauce. Combine all the sauce ingredients in a deep bowl. Cook, uncovered, 2-3 minutes on HIGH or until the sauce thickens and clears. Pour over the Egg Foo Yung to serve.

Cantonese Shrimp

PREPARATION TIME: 10 minutes

COOKING TIME: 15 minutes

SERVES: 4 people

3 tbsps salad or olive oil
2 cloves garlic, finely crushed
1lb peeled medium shrimp
2 inches root ginger, peeled and finely chopped
1 cup uncooked pork or bacon, finely chopped

Facing page: Cantonese Lobster.

minutes, without stirring, until it sets. Spoon the egg mixture over the shrimp. Alternatively, add the shrimp along with the beaten eggs. Allow the eggs to set and then mix gently. Serve at once.

Boiled Shrimp

PREPARATION TIME: 5 minutes, plus 10 minutes for the sauce

COOKING TIME: 10-15 minutes

SERVES: 6 people

SAUCE
2½ tbsps dark soy sauce
3½ tbsps light soy sauce
½ inch fresh root ginger, peeled and shredded
2 green onions, finely chopped
1 red chili, seeded and shredded
4 tbsps cooked oil
2 tsps ketchup

2lbs medium or large uncooked shrimp in their shells
Salt

Mix the sauce ingredients together. Wash the shrimp and drain. Place the shrimp into a wire basket and lower into a large pan of boiling, salted water. Boil for 10-12 minutes. Drain. Serve the drained hot shrimps with small bowls of sauce for dipping.

Shrimp and Ginger

PREPARATION TIME: 10 minutes

COOKING TIME: 10 minutes

SERVES: 4-6 people

2 tbsps salad or olive oil
1½lbs peeled medium shrimp
1 inch fresh root ginger, peeled and finely chopped
2 cloves garlic, peeled and finely chopped
2-3 green onions, chopped lengthwise into 1 inch pieces
1 leek, white part only, cut into strips.
1 cup shelled peas, lightly cooked
2 cups bean sprouts

SEASONING
2½ tbsps dark soy sauce

SAUCE
1¼ tbsps rice wine or dry sherry
1¼ tbsps light soy sauce
1 tsp fine granulated sugar
1 cup broth or water
1 tbsp cornstarch mixed with 2 tbsps broth or water

2-3 green onions, chopped
2 eggs, lightly beaten

Heat 1 tbsp oil in a wok. Add the garlic and fry for 1 minute. Add the shrimp and stir-fry for 4-5 minutes. Remove to

This page: Shrimp with Pea Pods and Corn. Facing page: Shrimp and Ginger (top), Boiled Shrimp (center) and Cantonese Shrimp (page 56) (bottom).

a dish. Keep warm. Add the remaining oil to the wok and fry the ginger and pork for 3-4 minutes until it loses its color. Add the mixed sauce ingredients to the wok and cook for 1 minute. Add the onions and cook for 1 minute. Add the beaten eggs and cook for 1-2

1 tsp fine granulated sugar
Pinch monosodium glutamate (optional)
Pinch of salt

Heat the oil in a wok and stir-fry the
shrimp for 2-3 minutes. Remove the
shrimp to a dish. Reheat the oil and
add the ginger and garlic and fry for 1
minute. Add the onions and stir-fry for
1 minute. Add the leek, peas and bean
sprouts. Stir fry for 2-3 minutes.
Sprinkle over the seasoning ingredients
and return the shrimp to the wok.
Cover and cook for 2 minutes. Serve
immediately.

Shrimp with Pea Pods and Corn

PREPARATION TIME: 20 minutes

MICROWAVE COOKING TIME:
5-8 minutes

SERVES: 4 people

1½ lbs shelled jumbo shrimp, uncooked
3 tbsps oil
1 clove garlic, minced
1 small piece ginger root, minced
4 tbsps light stock
4 tbsps light soy sauce
4 tbsps rice wine
2 tsps cornstarch
2 tbsps Chinese parsley
2oz pea pods
4oz baby ears of corn
Salt

Heat a browning dish for 5 minutes
on HIGH. Shell and de-vein the
shrimp if necessary. Add the oil to
the dish and the shrimp. Add the
garlic and ginger and cook for 1-2
minutes on HIGH, stirring often.
Combine the stock, soy sauce, wine
and cornstarch. Pour over the shrimp
and cook for 3-4 minutes on
MEDIUM, stirring halfway through
the cooking time. Cut the stalks off
the pea pods and add with the ears of
corn to the dish. Cut the corn in half
lengthwise if the ears are large. Cook
for 1-2 minutes on MEDIUM, until
the sauce thickens and clears. If the
shrimp are cooked after 3-4 minutes,
remove them before adding the
vegetables. Serve with rice or
noodles.

aside. Combine the remaining ingredients, except the peas, in a deep bowl. Cook for 2-3 minutes on HIGH, or until the sauce thickens, stirring after 1 minute. Add the shrimp, lower the setting to MEDIUM and cook for about 3 minutes. Check the shrimp after 2 minutes. They must not overcook or they will toughen. Add the frozen peas during the last 1 minute of cooking. Add salt if necessary and serve with rice or noodles.

Shrimp with Cashew Nuts

PREPARATION TIME: 10 minutes

COOKING TIME: 7-8 minutes

SERVES: 4 people

3 tbsps salad or olive oil
¾ cup cashew nuts
2 tsp cornstarch
1 cup chicken broth or water
1 onion, peeled and cut into small pieces
⅓ cup sliced green beans
⅔ cup Chinese cabbage, or white cabbage, shredded
½ cup bamboo shoots, sliced
1lb peeled medium shrimp
Salt and freshly ground black pepper to taste
4 rings pineapple, cut into chunks
Pinch monosodium glutamate (optional)

Heat 1 tbsp oil in a wok and stir-fry the cashew nuts until light brown. Remove the nuts and keep on one side. Mix the cornstarch with 2 tbsps water or broth and keep on one side. Reheat the wok with the remaining oil and fry the onion for 1 minute. Add the beans, cabbage and bamboo shoots and stir-fry for 2-3 minutes. Add the cashew nuts and shrimp and then add the remaining broth, salt and pepper, and the pineapple. Simmer for 1 minute and then add the MSG and cornstarch mixture and cook until the sauce thickens. Serve immediately.

Shrimp with Peas

PREPARATION TIME: 15 minutes

MICROWAVE COOKING TIME: 3 minutes plus 2 minutes standing time

SERVES: 4 people

1½ lbs shelled jumbo shrimp
1 tbsp cornstarch
2 tbsps rice wine
⅓ cup light stock
2 tbsps light soy sauce
Dash sesame oil
½ cup frozen peas

Shell and de-vein the shrimp and set

This page: Shrimp and Cauliflower (page 63) (top right), Shrimp with Cashew Nuts (center left) and Pea Pods with Shrimp (page 63) (bottom).

Pineapple Shrimp with Peppers

PREPARATION TIME: 20 minutes

MICROWAVE COOKING TIME:
6-7 minutes

SERVES: 4 people

SAUCE
Pineapple Sauce recipe with
2 tbsps rice wine
2 tbsps light soy sauce
1 large green pepper, cut in thin strips

1½ lbs shelled jumbo shrimp, de-veined
3 tbsps oil

Add the rice wine and soy sauce to
the Pineapple Sauce recipe. If the
sauce is still too thick, thin with a
spoonful of water. Heat a browning
dish 5 minutes on HIGH. Pour in the
oil and add the shrimp. Cook 1
minute on HIGH. Pour over the
sauce, add the strips of pepper and
cook 3 minutes on MEDIUM. Do
not overcook or shrimp will toughen.
Serve with rice.

Crispy Fish with Chili

PREPARATION TIME: 40 minutes

COOKING TIME: 30 minutes

SERVES: 4 people

1lb fish fillets, skinned, bones removed,
*   and cut into 1" cubes*

BATTER
4 tbsps flour
1 egg, separated
1 tbsp oil
5 tbsps milk
Salt

SAUCE
1 tsp grated ginger root
¼ tsp chili powder
2 tbsps tomato paste
2 tbsps tomato relish
2 tbsps dark soy sauce
2 tbsps Chinese wine or dry sherry
2 tbsps water
1 tsp sugar
1 red chili pepper, seeds removed, and
*   sliced finely*

1 clove garlic, crushed
Salt
Pepper
Oil for deep frying

Sift the flour with a pinch of salt.
Make a well in the center, and drop
in the egg yolk and oil. Mix to a
smooth batter with the milk,
gradually incorporating the flour.
Beat well. Cover and set aside in a
cool place for 30 minutes. Whisk egg
white until stiff, and fold into batter
just before using. Heat oil in wok.
Dip fish pieces into batter and coat
completely. When oil is hot, carefully

lower fish pieces in and cook until
cooked through and golden brown –
about 10 minutes. Remove with a
slotted spoon. Reheat oil and refry
each fish piece for 2 minutes.
Remove with a slotted spoon and
drain on paper towels. Carefully
remove all but 1 tbsp of oil from wok.
Heat oil, and add chili pepper, ginger,
garlic, chili powder, tomato paste,
tomato relish, soy sauce, sugar, wine
and water, and salt and pepper to
taste. Stir well over heat for 3
minutes. Increase heat and toss in
fish pieces. Coat with sauce and,
when heated through, serve
immediately.

Shrimp and Cauliflower

PREPARATION TIME: 15 minutes	
COOKING TIME: 14-15 minutes	
SERVES: 4-6 people	

3 tbsps salad or olive oil
1 clove garlic, peeled and finely chopped
1lb medium size shrimp, peeled
10oz cauliflower flowerets, cut into smaller
  pieces
1 cup water or broth
Salt to taste
1½ cups shelled peas, lightly cooked

SAUCE
2 tsps cornstarch
2 tbsps broth or water
Freshly ground black pepper to taste

Heat the oil in a wok and fry the garlic
for 2 minutes. Add the shrimp and
cook for 3 minutes. Remove the
shrimp. Add the cauliflower and fry for
2-3 minutes, stirring constantly. Add
broth, cover and simmer for five
minutes. Add salt to taste and the peas
and cook for a further 2-3 minutes.
Return the shrimp to the wok and stir
well. Add the blended sauce
ingredients and gently simmer until it
thickens. Serve immediately.

Pea Pods with Shrimp

PREPARATION TIME: 10 minutes	
COOKING TIME: 6-8 minutes	
SERVES: 4-6 people	

1 tsp cornstarch
1 tsp fine granulated sugar
1 tsp dark soy sauce
1 tbsp water
3 tbsps salad or olive oil
1lb peeled medium size shrimp
1 cup chicken broth
½ tsp salt

**Facing page: Squid with Broccoli and
Cauliflower (page 66). This page:
Ginger Scallops in Oyster Sauce (page
64) (top) and Crispy Fish with Chili
(bottom).**

1⅓ cups pea pods
¾ cup water chestnuts, sliced
1 small onion, peeled and cut into small
    pieces
1 stem celery, cut into ¼ inch pieces
Pinch monosodium glutamate (optional)

Mix together the cornstarch, sugar, soy sauce and water. Heat the oil in a wok. Add the shrimp and stir-fry for 2 minutes. Add the broth, salt, pea pods, water chestnuts, onions and celery. Cover and cook for 2 minutes. Stir in the monosodium glutamate. Stir in the cornstarch mixture and simmer gently until the sauce thickens. Serve as a side dish.

Ginger Scallops in Oyster Sauce

PREPARATION TIME: 10 minutes

COOKING TIME: 15 minutes

SERVES: 4 people

1lb scallops, cleaned, dried on absorbent
    paper, and sliced
10 green onions, sliced diagonally into
    1″ slices
1″ green ginger, peeled and sliced very
    thinly
Salt
2 tbsps vegetable oil

SAUCE
1 tbsp oyster sauce
1 tbsp light soy sauce
½ tsp sesame oil
1 tsp grated root ginger
1 tsp cornstarch
5 tbsps light stock, or 5 tbsps hot water
    and half a chicken bouillon cube
Pinch of sugar

Combine oyster sauce, soy sauce, sesame oil, cornstarch, sugar and grated ginger and set aside. Sprinkle the scallops with a pinch of salt. Heat wok, and add oil. Add sliced ginger and green onions, and stir-fry gently for 1 minute. Raise heat to high. Add scallops and stir-fry for 1 minute. Add sauce mixture and stir in. Remove from heat, and stir in stock gradually. Return to heat and bring to the boil, stirring continuously. Simmer gently for 3 minutes, until sauce is slightly thickened. Adjust seasoning. Serve immediately with boiled rice.

Steamed Fish in Ginger

PREPARATION TIME: 20 minutes

COOKING TIME: 15 minutes

SERVES: 4 people

3lbs whole snapper, bass or bream,
    cleaned and scaled

STUFFING
½ cup cooked rice
1 tsp grated root ginger
3 green onions, sliced finely
2 tsps light soy sauce
6 green onions, cut into 2″ lengths, then
    into fine shreds
3 pieces green ginger, cut into fine shreds

GARNISH
Lemon slices and parsley, if desired

Mix together rice, grated ginger, sliced green onion and soy sauce. Stuff rice mixture into cleaned fish cavity, packing in well. Place fish on a heat-proof plate, and arrange strips of green onion and green ginger on top of fish. Put the plate on top of a bamboo steamer or metal trivet standing in wok. Add water, ensuring the water level is not up to the plate. Cover and bring to the boil. Steam for 10 minutes from boiling point. Ensure that the fish is cooked, but be sure not to oversteam the fish. Serve hot, garnished with lemon slices and parsley, if desired.

Honey Sesame Shrimp

PREPARATION TIME: 20 minutes

COOKING TIME: 20 minutes

SERVES: 4 people

1lb shrimp, shelled and de-veined
2 tbsps cornstarch
¾ cup flour
½ tsp baking powder
1 egg, lightly beaten
Pinch of salt
Pepper
⅔ cup water
Oil for deep frying
2 tbsps honey
1 tbsp sesame seeds
1 tbsp sesame oil

Sift flour, baking powder and salt and pepper into a bowl. Make a well in the center and add egg and water,

Honey Sesame Shrimp (top) and Steamed Fish in Ginger (right).

gradually bringing in the flour. Beat to a smooth batter and set aside for 10 minutes. Meanwhile, toss shrimp in cornstarch and coat well. Shake off any excess cornstarch. Add shrimp to batter and coat well. Heat oil in wok, and add shrimp, a few at a time. Cook until batter is golden. Remove and drain on paper towels, and keep warm. Repeat until all shrimp have been fried. Carefully remove hot oil from wok. Gently heat sesame oil in pan. Add honey and stir until mixed well and heated through. Add shrimp to mixture and toss well. Sprinkle over sesame seeds and again toss well. Serve immediately.

Squid with Broccoli and Cauliflower

PREPARATION TIME: 15 minutes

COOKING TIME: 20 minutes

SERVES: 4 people

1lb squid, cleaned
1 onion, peeled and chopped roughly
8oz fresh broccoli flowerets
8oz fresh cauliflower flowerets
2 sticks celery, sliced diagonally
½ tsp grated ginger root
1 tbsp cornstarch
2 tbsps water
2 tbsps light soy sauce
2 tbsps Chinese wine, or dry sherry
2 tbsps oyster sauce
½ tsp sesame oil
½ tsp sugar
⅔ cup oil, for deep frying
Salt
Pepper

Cut cleaned squid lengthwise down center. Flatten out with inside uppermost. With a sharp knife make a lattice design, cutting deep into squid flesh (to tenderize and make squid curl when cooking). Heat oil in wok. Add squid and cook until it curls. Remove from pan and drain on paper towels. Carefully pour off all

but 1 tbsp of oil. Add onion, celery, broccoli, cauliflower and ginger, and stir-fry for 3 minutes. Slake cornstarch with water, and add soy sauce, wine, oyster sauce, sesame oil, sugar, and salt and pepper to taste. Mix well and add to wok. Bring to the boil and simmer for 3 minutes, stirring continuously. Return squid and cook until heated through. Place in a warm serving dish and serve hot with rice.

Embroidered Crabmeat Balls

PREPARATION TIME: 25 minutes

MICROWAVE COOKING TIME: 5-6 minutes

SERVES: 4-6 people

1lb crabmeat
2-3 egg whites
1 tsp salt
Pinch pepper
1 tbsp sherry
1 tbsp cornstarch
½ green pepper, finely chopped
¼ red pepper, finely chopped
2 tbsps finely chopped ham
2 green onions, finely chopped
3 large leaves Chinese cabbage, chopped
½ tsp ground ginger
1 cup hot chicken stock
2 tbsps cornstarch
2 tbsps light soy sauce
Dash sesame oil

Mix the first 11 ingredients, adding only 2 egg whites. If the mixture is dry and crumbly, add some of the remaining white until the mixture will hold together. Shape into 1 inch balls. The balls should not be smooth. Place in a single layer in a large, shallow dish. Pour around the hot stock and cover the dish. Cook 3 minutes on HIGH, rearranging the balls once during cooking to bring the ones in the center of the dish to the outside. Remove the balls and

keep warm. Mix the remaining cornstarch with the soy sauce in a glass measure and gradually add the stock. Stir well and cook 2-3 minutes on HIGH, until thickened. Add the sesame oil and pour over the crabmeat balls to serve.

Squid with Shrimp and Tomatoes

PREPARATION TIME: 25 minutes

MICROWAVE COOKING TIME: 4-5 minutes

SERVES: 4 people

8oz squid, cleaned
8oz shrimp, peeled
2 tbsps oil

SAUCE
¾ cup stock
2 tbsps rice wine
1 tbsp soy sauce
2 tbsps tomato paste
1 tbsp cornstarch
¼ tsp ground ginger
Salt and pepper
4 tomatoes, peeled and sliced

Heat the oil in a casserole dish for 30 seconds on HIGH. Cut the squid into rings and add to the oil with the shrimp. Stir to coat and cook, covered, on MEDIUM for 2 minutes. Set aside. If using cooked shrimp, add to the squid after 2 minutes. Combine all the sauce ingredients, except the tomatoes. Cook for 2-3 minutes on HIGH or until sauce has thickened. Add the tomatoes and pour over the squid. Leave to stand a few minutes to reheat the seafood. Serve with rice.

Facing page: Squid with Shrimp and Tomatoes (top) and Embroidered Crabmeat Balls (bottom).

MEAT DISHES

Beef with Broccoli

PREPARATION TIME: 20 minutes

MICROWAVE COOKING TIME:
7-8 minutes

SERVES: 4 people

1lb rump steak, cut in thin strips
3 tbsps oil
¼ cup soy sauce
1 tbsp cornstarch
1 tbsp sherry
1 tsp sugar
⅓ cup stock
½ bunch broccoli
2 tsps grated ginger root
Salt and pepper

Heat a browning dish 5 minutes on HIGH. Mix the beef and oil and add to the dish. Cook 2 minutes on HIGH in 2 or 3 batches. Slice the stalks of the broccoli thinly on the diagonal. Separate the flowerets into small pieces. Toss in the oil with the meat and cook for 1 minute on HIGH. Leave to stand covered while preparing the sauce. Mix the soy sauce, cornstarch, sherry, sugar and ginger root in a small bowl. Cook 2-3 minutes on HIGH, until thickened. Stir several times after 1 minute's cooking. Pour over the beef and broccoli. Cook a further 1 minute on HIGH. Adjust the seasoning and serve immediately with rice or noodles.

Sweet and Sour Pork and Pineapple

PREPARATION TIME: 20 minutes

COOKING TIME: 45 minutes

SERVES: 4 people

1lb pork tenderloin, cut into 1" cubes
1 clove garlic, crushed
1 tsp grated ginger root
2 tbsps light soy sauce
1 tbsp cornstarch
2 tbsps peanut oil
⅔ cup water
2 tbsps white wine vinegar
2 tbsps tomato paste
1 tbsp sugar
1 can pineapple chunks, drained

GARNISH
Fresh coriander

This page: **Beef with Broccoli. Facing page: Sweet and Sour Pork and Pineapple.**

Place pork in bowl. Pour over light soy sauce and toss together. Leave for 15 minutes. Make sauce. Mix together vinegar, tomato paste and sugar, and set aside. Heat wok and add oil. Remove pork from soy sauce, and add soy sauce to sauce mixture. Toss pork in cornstarch, coating well. When oil is hot, brown pork well all

over. Remove from pan and reduce heat. Fry garlic and ginger for 30 seconds. Add water. Bring to the boil, then return pork to wok. Reduce heat; cover and simmer for 15 minutes, stirring occasionally. Add sauce mixture and pineapple, and simmer for a further 15 minutes. Garnish with coriander. Serve hot with rice or noodles.

Steak Chinese Style

PREPARATION TIME:
1 hour 15 minutes

COOKING TIME: 20 minutes

SERVES: 4 people

8oz sirloin or butt steak, cut into 1" pieces
1 can straw mushrooms, drained
2 green onions, sliced diagonally into
*   ½" pieces*
2 cloves garlic, crushed
1 can baby corn, drained
½ tsp crushed ginger
1 tbsp oyster sauce
1 tbsp light soy sauce
2 tbsps dark soy sauce
2 tsps sugar
1 tsp sesame oil
1 tsp Chinese wine, or 2 tsps dry sherry
1 tsp cornstarch
¼ cup water
Pinch of baking soda
3 tbsps peanut oil
Salt
Pepper

GARNISH
Green onion flowers (cut green onions
*   into 2" lengths. Carefully cut into fine*
*   shreds, keeping one end intact, and then*
*   soak in cold water until curling)*

Put steak in a bowl and sprinkle over baking soda. Mix together light soy sauce, sesame oil, wine, half the sugar, half the cornstarch, and seasoning. Pour over the steak and leave for at least an hour, turning meat occasionally. Meanwhile, make sauce by mixing 2 tbsps of dark soy sauce, remaining sugar and cornstarch, and water. Mix together and set aside. Heat wok, add peanut oil and, when hot, fry steak for 4 minutes. Remove from wok and set aside. Add garlic, green onions, ginger, mushrooms,

baby corn, and finally steak. Add oyster sauce, and mix well. Then add sauce mixture and bring to the boil. Cook for 3 minutes, stirring occasionally. Serve hot with rice, garnished with green onion flowers.

Beef with Pineapple and Peppers

PREPARATION TIME: 40 minutes

COOKING TIME: 15 minutes

SERVES: 4 people

1lb sirloin or butt steak, sliced thinly
1 can pineapple slices, drained and
*   chopped*
1 green pepper, cored, seeds removed, and
*   chopped roughly*
1 red pepper, cored, seeds removed, and
*   chopped roughly*
2 cloves garlic, crushed
1 tsp chopped ginger root
1 onion, peeled and chopped roughly
2 tbsps light soy sauce
1 tsp sugar
2 tsps cornstarch
2 tbsps water
1 tbsp peanut oil

SAUCE
1 tbsp plum sauce
1 tbsp dark soy sauce
1 tsp sugar
1 tsp sesame oil
1 tsp cornstarch
¼ cup water
Salt
Pepper

Combine 2 tbsps of light soy sauce

Facing page: Steak Chinese Style. This page: Beef with Pineapple and Peppers.

with 1 tsp of sugar, 2 tsps of cornstarch and 2 tbsps of water. Mix well and pour over steak. Toss together well, and put aside for at least 30 minutes, turning occasionally. Heat wok and add peanut oil. Add ginger, garlic, onion and peppers, and stir-fry for 3 minutes. Remove from wok and set aside. Add extra oil if necessary and stir-fry beef, well separated, for 2 minutes. Remove from wok. Mix together all sauce ingredients in wok, and heat until sauce begins to thicken. Add vegetables, beef and pineapple, and toss together over a high heat until heated through. Serve with boiled rice.

Sliced Pork in Wine Sauce

PREPARATION TIME: 30 minutes

COOKING TIME: about 16 minutes

SERVES: 4 people

SEASONING

1¼ tbsps wine-flavored vinegar
1¼ tbsps light soy sauce
1 tbsp rice wine or dry sherry
2 tsps soy paste
1 tsp freshly ground black pepper
1 tsp salt
1 tsp Shao Hsing wine

1lb pork fillet, cut into 2 inch long, thin
   slices
1 tbsp cornstarch
4 tbsps salad or olive oil
½ inch fresh root ginger, finely chopped
3 green onions, chopped
1 green pepper, seeded and diced

SAUCE

2 tsps cornstarch
4 tbsps dry white wine
½ cup chicken broth
2 tsps dark soy sauce
1 tsp fine granulated sugar
½ tsp salt

Mix the seasoning ingredients together. Add the pork slices and leave to marinate for 10-15 minutes. Drain the pork and roll in the cornstarch. Leave on one side. Discard the marinade. Heat half the oil in the wok until smoking. Add the pork, reduce the heat, and stir-fry for 4-6 minutes until lightly browned. Remove the pork and keep on one side. Discard any oil left in the wok. Add the remaining oil to the wok and stir-fry the onions, ginger and green pepper for 3-5 minutes. Return the fried pork to the wok and cook for a further 2-3 minutes with the vegetables. Remove onto a serving dish. Mix the cornstarch from the sauce ingredients with 2 tbsps water. Add the remaining sauce ingredients to the wok and bring to the boil. Add the blended cornstarch. Stir and simmer until the sauce thickens, simmer for 1-2 minutes. Pour over the pork and serve.

Pork-Stuffed Mushrooms

PREPARATION TIME: 15-20 minutes

COOKING TIME: 12 minutes

SERVES: 4 people

FILLING

1 egg
2 tsps cornstarch
2 tsps rice wine or dry sherry
¼ tsp minced fresh root ginger
6 water chestnuts, finely chopped
½ cup peeled medium shrimp, chopped
1½ cups ground lean pork
¼ tsp salt
¼ tsp freshly ground black pepper
½ tsp fine granulated sugar
2 tsps chili sauce

16 large, open mushrooms
2½ cups chicken broth
Oil

Mix all the filling ingredients together. Remove the mushroom stalks. Divide the filling into 16 portions. Bring the chicken broth to the boil. Add the

mushrooms and leave to stand off the heat for 5 minutes, covered. Drain the mushrooms and discard the broth. Top each mushroom with a portion of filling. Put the stuffed mushrooms into a well-oiled steamer. Steam for 10-12 minutes over boiling water. Serve as a snack, as a starter or as a side dish. Alternatively, serve with a simple sauce made from thickened chicken broth. Pour the sauce over the steamed mushrooms.

Diced Pork with Corn (page 74) (far left), Sliced Pork in Wine Sauce (left) and Pork-Stuffed Mushrooms (below).

Heat a browning dish for 5 minutes on HIGH. Mix meat and oil and add to the dish. Cook for 2 minutes on HIGH, stirring often. Combine the yellow beans, soy sauce, wine, cornstarch and stock. Mix very well and pour over the pork. Cover the dish or transfer to a covered casserole and cook for 5-7 minutes on MEDIUM, stirring halfway through the cooking time. Cook on HIGH for 2 minutes until thickened. Add the pepper and bamboo shoots and cook a further 1 minute on HIGH. Serve with rice or noodles.

Diced Pork with Corn

PREPARATION TIME: 25 minutes
COOKING TIME: 15-20 minutes
SERVES: 2 people

MARINADE
Pinch salt
2½ tsps dark soy sauce
¼ tsp fine granulated sugar
1 tsp rice wine
1 tbsp water

1½ cups pork loin, diced
Oil for deep frying
2 slices fresh root ginger, peeled and diced
1 clove garlic, peeled and chopped
1 cup chicken broth

SEASONING
¼ tsp salt
¼ tsp freshly ground black pepper
¼ tsp fine granulated sugar
1 tsp rice wine or dry sherry
Few drops sesame oil
1 tsp cornstarch mixed with 1 tbsp water

1 cup canned creamed corn
1 egg, well beaten
4 green onions, chopped

Mix the marinade ingredients together. Add the pork and leave to marinate for 15 minutes. Drain the pork and discard the liquid. Heat the wok and pour in

Jade and Ivory Pork

PREPARATION TIME: 30 minutes
MICROWAVE COOKING TIME:
10-12 minutes
SERVES: 4 people

1lb pork tenderloin, cut in very fine strips
3 tbsps oil

3 tbsps yellow beans
4 tbsps light soy sauce
2 tbsps rice wine
1 tbsp cornstarch
¾ cup chicken stock
8oz can bamboo shoots, cut in strips if necessary
1 large green pepper, cut in strips about the same size as bamboo shoots

This page: Beef and Oyster Sauce (page 80). Facing page: Jade and Ivory Pork.

the oil for deep frying. Fry the pork until light brown. Remove the pork and drain. Reserve the oil for future use. Heat 1 tbsp oil in the wok and add the ginger and pork. Stir-fry for 3 minutes. Add the broth and simmer for 3 minutes. Add the seasoning ingredients and simmer for 2-3 minutes. Add the blended cornstarch and water and simmer until the sauce thickens. Add the corn and beaten egg and cook for 2-3 minutes. Serve sprinkled with chopped onions. Serve this dish with plain boiled rice or noodles.

Pink and Silver Pork

PREPARATION TIME: 15 minutes

MICROWAVE COOKING TIME: 11-16 minutes

SERVES: 4 people

8oz pork tenderloin, cut into thin shreds
8oz ham, cut into thin strips
1 cup light stock
4 tbsps rice wine
2 tbsps light soy sauce
1 clove garlic, finely minced
1 small piece fresh ginger root, grated
1 tbsp cornstarch mixed with 2 tbsps
   water
4oz bean sprouts

Combine all the ingredients, except the bean sprouts, in a large casserole dish and cover. Cook for 10-15 minutes on MEDIUM, stirring halfway through the cooking time. Add the bean sprouts and cook a further 1 minute on HIGH. Leave to stand 2 minutes before serving.

Beef with Mango

PREPARATION TIME: 20 minutes

COOKING TIME: 15 minutes

SERVES: 4 people

1lb sirloin or butt steak, sliced thinly
1 can mangoes, drained, reserving ¼ cup
   mango juice
1 tsp sugar
½ tsp salt
1 tsp cornstarch
Pinch of pepper
2 tbsps mango chutney

1 tbsp plum sauce
1 tbsp oil

Combine 2 tbsps mango juice, sugar, cornstarch, salt and pepper, and pour over steak. Toss well and set aside for 15 minutes. Mix remaining mango juice with mango chutney and plum sauce, and set aside. Chop finely half of the mangoes and add to the sauce, retaining enough slices for decoration. Heat wok and add oil. Stir-fry steak for 5 minutes, tossing well, or until browned all over. Add mango-plum sauce and cook for a further 5 minutes. Decorate dish with reserved mango slices. Serve with rice.

Pork in Plum Sauce with Almonds

PREPARATION TIME: 30 minutes

MICROWAVE COOKING TIME: 11-18 minutes

SERVES: 4 people

SAUCE
Plum Sauce recipe
1 purple or red plum, thinly sliced
1lb pork tenderloin, cut in thin slices
2 tbsps oil
2 tbsps soy sauce

GARNISH
½ cup toasted whole almonds

Facing page: Pink and Silver Pork (top) and Pork in Plum Sauce with Almonds (bottom). This page: Beef with Mango.

When the plum sauce is ready, add the thinly sliced plum, keep the bowl covered and set aside while preparing the pork. Heat a browning dish for 5 minutes on HIGH. Pour in the oil and add the pork. Cook for 2 minutes on HIGH, stirring often.

Add the soy sauce, cover the dish and cook for 5-7 minutes more on MEDIUM. When the pork is tender, pour over the plum sauce and heat for 1 minute on HIGH. Serve sprinkled with the toasted almonds.

Pork Spare Ribs

PREPARATION TIME: 25 minutes
COOKING TIME: 40-45 minutes
SERVES: 4 people

16-20 pork spare ribs
1 tsp salt
Salad or olive oil
1 tsp ginger paste
1 tsp garlic paste
1 tsp onion paste
Pinch monosodium glutamate (optional)
1 tsp light soy sauce
1 tsp cornstarch
1 egg
½ tsp Shao Hsing wine
½ tsp chili oil

SAUCE
3 tbsps brown sugar
3 tbsps black vinegar
1 tbsp ketchup
1 tsp cornstarch
1 tsp water

1 tbsp dark soy sauce
½ tsp salt
½ tsp freshly ground black pepper

Trim excess fat from spare ribs and rub with salt. Add 4 tbsps oil to the wok and fry the ginger, garlic and onion for 1-2 minutes. Add the spare ribs and stir-fry for 6 minutes. Remove to a dish and add the monosodium glutamate, light soy sauce, cornstarch, egg, wine and chili oil. Marinate for 10 minutes. Prepare the sauce by mixing all the ingredients together in the wok and bringing them gently to the boil. Simmer for 2-3 minutes and add the spare ribs along with their marinade. Stir-fry until the liquid is reduced to half its original quantity. Put all the ingredients onto a baking tray and spread out evenly. Bake at 375°F for 25 minutes. Baste occasionally with the liquid from the tray and oil. The spare ribs should have browned well and be well coated with seasoning. Serve hot or cold.

**Pork Meatballs in Sauce (left),
Pork Spare Ribs (above) and
Barbecued Pork (page 80) (right).**

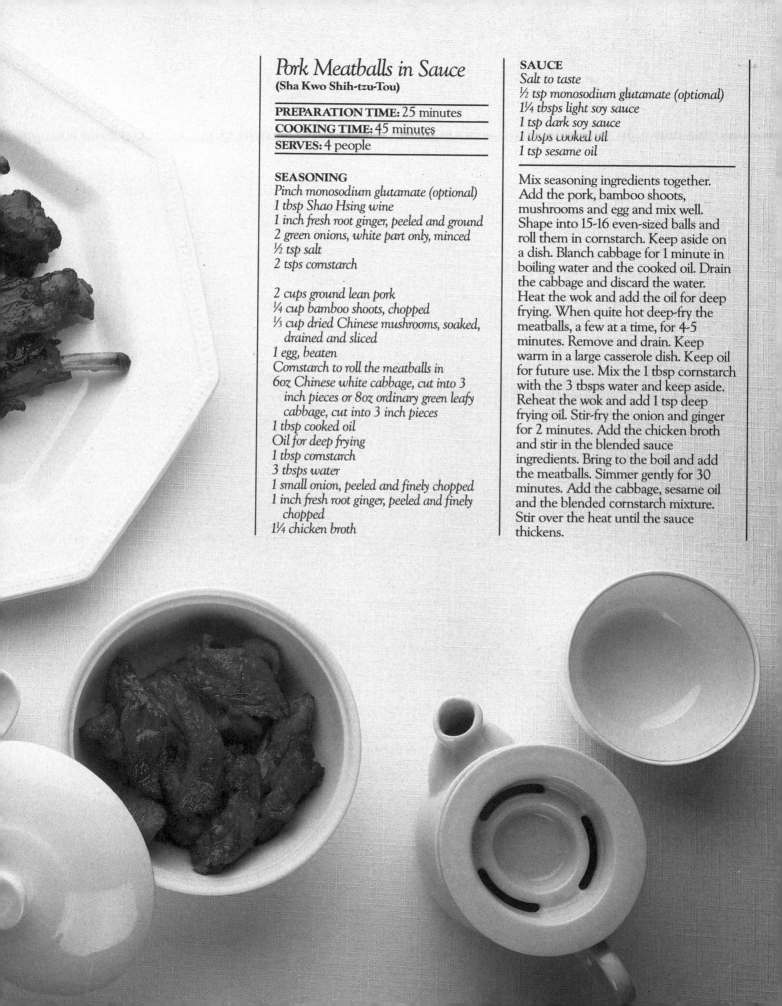

Pork Meatballs in Sauce
(Sha Kwo Shih-tzu-Tou)

PREPARATION TIME: 25 minutes
COOKING TIME: 45 minutes
SERVES: 4 people

SEASONING
Pinch monosodium glutamate (optional)
1 tbsp Shao Hsing wine
1 inch fresh root ginger, peeled and ground
2 green onions, white part only, minced
½ tsp salt
2 tsps cornstarch

2 cups ground lean pork
¼ cup bamboo shoots, chopped
⅓ cup dried Chinese mushrooms, soaked,
   drained and sliced
1 egg, beaten
Cornstarch to roll the meatballs in
6oz Chinese white cabbage, cut into 3
   inch pieces or 8oz ordinary green leafy
   cabbage, cut into 3 inch pieces
1 tbsp cooked oil
Oil for deep frying
1 tbsp cornstarch
3 tbsps water
1 small onion, peeled and finely chopped
1 inch fresh root ginger, peeled and finely
   chopped
1¼ chicken broth

SAUCE
Salt to taste
½ tsp monosodium glutamate (optional)
1¼ tbsps light soy sauce
1 tsp dark soy sauce
1 tbsps cooked oil
1 tsp sesame oil

Mix seasoning ingredients together.
Add the pork, bamboo shoots,
mushrooms and egg and mix well.
Shape into 15-16 even-sized balls and
roll them in cornstarch. Keep aside on
a dish. Blanch cabbage for 1 minute in
boiling water and the cooked oil. Drain
the cabbage and discard the water.
Heat the wok and add the oil for deep
frying. When quite hot deep-fry the
meatballs, a few at a time, for 4-5
minutes. Remove and drain. Keep
warm in a large casserole dish. Keep oil
for future use. Mix the 1 tbsp cornstarch
with the 3 tbsps water and keep aside.
Reheat the wok and add 1 tsp deep
frying oil. Stir-fry the onion and ginger
for 2 minutes. Add the chicken broth
and stir in the blended sauce
ingredients. Bring to the boil and add
the meatballs. Simmer gently for 30
minutes. Add the cabbage, sesame oil
and the blended cornstarch mixture.
Stir over the heat until the sauce
thickens.

Beef with Tree Ears

PREPARATION TIME: 30 minutes

MICROWAVE COOKING TIME:
7-8 minutes

SERVES: 4 people

8 pieces dried black fungi (tree or wood ears)
1lb rump steak, cut in thin strips
3 tbsps oil
4 tbsps soy sauce
1 tbsp rice wine
2 tsps chili sauce (sweet or hot)
⅓ cup stock
1 tbsp cornstarch
1 small bunch chives, chopped

Soak the tree ears for 20 minutes in hot water. Heat a browning dish for 5 minutes on HIGH. Combine oil and meat and add to the dish. Cook 2 minutes on HIGH in 2 or 3 batches. Re-heat dish 2 minutes after each batch. Drain the tree ears well and add whole to the steak in the browning dish. Cook 1 minute on HIGH, turning once. Mix the remaining ingredients, except the chives, together and pour over the meat and tree ears. Cook 2-3 minutes on HIGH, until the sauce thickens and clears. Sprinkle over the chopped chives before serving.

Barbecued Pork
(Kan Hsiang Ch'a Shao or Char Siu)

PREPARATION TIME: 3 hours

COOKING TIME: 1 hour to 1 hour 30 minutes

SERVES: 6-8 people

4½lbs loin of pork

SEASONING
1 tbsp ginger juice
Few drops red food coloring
5 tbsps brown sugar
1 cup light soy sauce
1 tsp salt
1 tbsp Mue Kwe Lo wine (or a mixture of 2 tsps dry sherry and 1 tsp apricot brandy)

8oz honey, melted

Remove the bones from the loin of pork. Cut pork into 1½ inch wide strips. With the aid of a fork scrape the surface of the pork lightly to form grooves in which the seasoning can lodge. Mix the seasoning ingredients together and rub well into the pork strips. Leave to marinate for at least 1½ hours. Thread the pork strips onto a long metal skewer and hang to dry for 1 hour. Put the pork onto a wire rack in a roasting pan. Brush with melted honey and roast in the oven at 350°F, for 1-1½ hours, basting with honey frequently. When cooked, brush the pork with any remaining honey and leave to 'dry' slightly. Serve hot or cold, sliced thinly on a serving plate.

Steamed Beef Balls with Two Different Mushrooms

PREPARATION TIME: 30 minutes

MICROWAVE COOKING TIME:
11-14 minutes

SERVES: 4-6 people

20 dried Chinese mushrooms
12oz ground beef
3 tbsps light soy sauce
2 tsps dry sherry
2 tsps grated fresh ginger root
Salt and pepper
24 fresh or frozen shelled peas
12-14oz Chinese straw mushrooms or small button mushrooms
2 tbsps cornstarch dissolved in 3 tbsps water

Soak the dried mushrooms for 30 minutes in hot water. Combine the ground beef, half the soy sauce, sherry, ginger, salt and pepper and shape into 24 small balls. Press one pea into the top of each beef ball. Arrange in a glass dish with space between each ball if possible. Combine the remaining soy sauce with 1 cup water. Pour over the beef balls and cover loosely with plastic wrap film. Cook on HIGH for 8-10 minutes. Turn the beef balls over and rearrange them once or twice during cooking. Make sure that those in the center are brought to the outside of

the dish. When the beef balls are cooked, remove to a serving dish and keep warm. Arrange in rows or in a circle, pea-side up. Skim the fat from the top of the cooking liquid. Combine the cornstarch with a spoonful of liquid. Stir into the remaining liquid in the dish and mix well. Cook for 2-3 minutes on HIGH, stirring after 1 minute. Add the two different mushrooms and cook until the sauce thickens. Arrange the mushrooms on the serving dish, keeping the two different kinds separate. Pour over the sauce to serve.

Beef and Oyster Sauce

PREPARATION TIME: 30 minutes

COOKING TIME: 20 minutes

SERVES: 4 people

1lb sirloin or butt steak, sliced into thin strips
1½ cups bean sprouts
½ cup button mushrooms
1 red pepper, cored, seeds removed, and chopped roughly
2 sticks celery, sliced diagonally
2 onions, peeled and quartered
2 tbsps light soy sauce
2 tbsps peanut or vegetable oil

OYSTER SAUCE
3 tbsps oyster sauce
1 chicken bouillon cube dissolved in 2 tbsps boiling water
1 tbsp dark soy sauce
1 tbsp Chinese wine or dry sherry
1 tbsp cornstarch
2 tbsps cold water
Salt
Pepper

Place steak in a bowl and pour over 2 tbsps light soy sauce. Toss together well and set aside for at least 30 minutes. Meanwhile, mix together oyster sauce, chicken stock, dark soy sauce and wine. Blend together cornstarch and cold water, and set

Facing page: Steamed Beef Balls with Two Different Mushrooms (top) and Beef with Tree Ears (bottom).

2 tbsps rice wine or dry sherry
1½ tbsps chili bean paste
2½ tbsps dark soy sauce
3-4 green onions, finely chopped
1lb fillet of beef, cut into 2 inch long strips
⅔ cup ground rice
1 large lotus leaf or several cabbage leaves

For the marinade, mix the ginger, salt,
sugar, pepper, oil, wine, bean paste, soy
sauce and half of the onions. Add beef
strips and mix well. Leave to marinate
for 15-20 minutes. Heat the wok and
dry-roast the ground rice for 2-4
minutes till rice changes color from
white to light brown. Roll the
marinated beef in the roasted ground
rice to give a thin, even coating. Line
the bamboo steamer with a well-oiled
lotus leaf or a few old and tough
cabbage leaves. Arrange the coated
beef strips in a neat pile on top. Steam
fairly quickly for 10-15 minutes over
boiling water. Garnish with the
remaining chopped onions before
serving. Serve hot with chili sauce.

Steamed Pork with Salted Cabbage

| **PREPARATION TIME:** 25 minutes |
| **COOKING TIME:** 2 hours |
| **SERVES:** 4 people |

1lb pork fillet cut into ½ inch thick slices
Salt
2 cups cabbage, shredded (Chinese white
    or plain green cabbage)

SEASONING
1 tbsp fine granulated sugar
2 tbsps cooked oil
1 tsp monosodium glutamate (optional)
4 tbsps broth or water
Salt and freshly ground black pepper

1¼ tbsps dark soy sauce
Oil for deep-frying

SAUCE
1 tsp cornstarch
1 tbsp water

Boil the pork in 2 cups water for ¾
hour until tender. Drain the pork and
discard the water. Boil 2 cups fresh
water with 1 tsp salt and add the

aside. Heat wok, and add oil. Add
onion, celery, mushrooms and red
pepper, and stir-fry for 5 minutes.
Remove from wok and set aside.
Reheat oil and, when hot, toss in
steak. Brown well all over, then add
sauce and fried vegetables. Add
cornstarch mixture and bring to the
boil, tossing continuously. Add salt
and pepper to taste. Finally, add bean
sprouts and simmer gently for
3 minutes. Serve hot with noodles or
rice.

Steamed Beef Szechuan Style

| **PREPARATION TIME:** 40 minutes |
| **COOKING TIME:** 15 minutes |
| **SERVES:** 4 people |

3 slices fresh root ginger, minced
1 tsp salt
1 tsp fine granulated sugar
Freshly ground black pepper
1 tbsp salad or olive oil

thickening of cornstarch and water. Stir over the heat until the sauce thickens. Pour over the cabbage and pork and serve.

Spiced Beef

PREPARATION TIME:	30 minutes
COOKING TIME:	5-6 minutes
SERVES:	4 people

MARINADE
1 tsp fine granulated sugar
2-3 star anise, ground
½ tsp ground fennel
1¼ tbsps dark soy sauce
¼ tsp monosodium glutamate (optional)

1lb fillet of beef, cut into 1 inch strips
1 inch fresh root ginger, peeled and crushed
½ tsp salt
2 tbsps salad or olive oil
4 green onions, sliced
½ tsp freshly ground black pepper
1¼ tbsps light soy sauce

Mix the marinade ingredients together. Add the beef strips, ginger and salt, and marinate for 20 minutes. Heat the oil in a wok and stir-fry the onions for 1 minute. Add beef, ground pepper and soy sauce and stir-fry for 4-5 minutes. Serve with a dip.

Beef with Green Pepper and Chili

PREPARATION TIME:	30 minutes
COOKING TIME:	10-12 minutes
SERVES:	4 people

1lb fillet of beef, cut into 1 inch strips

SEASONING
2 tbsps dark soy sauce
1 tsp sesame oil
Pinch baking soda
¼ tsp ground black pepper
½ tsp salt

Oil for frying
2 green peppers, seeded and thinly sliced
1 onion, peeled and sliced
2 green onions, chopped
1 inch fresh root ginger, peeled and sliced

cabbage. Cook for 2 minutes. Drain, rinse in cold water and then drain again. Season the cabbage with 1 tsp of the sugar and 1 tbsp of the cooked oil. Mix well and keep on one side. Place the pork in a dish and mix with the dark soy sauce. Leave for 10 minutes. Drain. Mix all the seasoning ingredients together. Heat the oil for deep-frying and fry the pork until it turns lightly golden. Drain and add to the seasoning mixture. Keep the oil for future use. Place the pork and the seasoning

Facing page: Steamed Pork with Salted Cabbage (top), Pork with Green Pepper (page 84) (center right) and Pork Chop Suey (page 88) (bottom). This page: Spiced Beef (top), Steamed Beef Szechuan Style (bottom left) and Beef with Green Pepper and Chili (bottom right).

mixture into a deep dish and put the boiled cabbage on top. Cover and steam over boiling water for 1 hour. Drain off any excess liquid and retain. Heat the wok and add the cabbage liquid. Add the blended sauce

2 garlic cloves, peeled and chopped
3 green chilies, sliced

SAUCE
2½ tbsps chicken broth
½ tsp monosodium glutamate (optional)
1½ tsps dark soy sauce
Salt to taste
Few drops sesame oil

Marinate beef with the seasoning ingredients for 15 minutes. Heat 2 tbsps oil in a wok and stir-fry green peppers and onions for 2 minutes. Remove to a plate. Reheat wok, add 2-3 tbsps oil and fry ginger, garlic, and green chilies for 1 minute. Add beef and stir-fry for 4-5 minutes. Add sauce ingredients, mixed together, and the fried peppers and onions. Stir-fry for a further 2 minutes and serve.

Pork Chow Mein

PREPARATION TIME: 20 minutes

COOKING TIME: 20 minutes

SERVES: 4 people

10oz egg noodles
1lb pork, sliced thinly
1 tbsp Chinese wine, or dry sherry
1 tsp grated root ginger
1 leek, sliced
1 red pepper, cored, seeds removed, and cut into strips
1 stick celery, sliced diagonally
2 tbsp peas
⅔ cup chicken or light stock
1 tbsp light soy sauce
1 tsp sugar
1 tsp cornstarch
1 tbsp water
1 small can bamboo shoots, sliced
3 tbsps oil
Salt
Pepper

Soak noodles in hot water for 8 minutes, or as directed. Rinse in cold water, and drain. Combine wine, soy sauce and sugar, and pour over pork. Toss together and set aside for at least 15 minutes. Heat wok and add oil. Add ginger, celery and leek, and stir-fry for 2 minutes. Add red pepper and bamboo shoots, and stir-fry for a further 2 minutes. Remove from wok. Increase heat, and add

pork, reserving marinade. Stir-fry over high heat for 4 minutes. Return vegetables to wok. Add chicken stock gradually and stir well. Add peas and cook for 2 minutes. Blend cornstarch with water. Mix into marinade sauce and stir well. Add noodles and sauce to wok and toss together, heating through as sauce thickens. Add salt and pepper to taste. Simmer for 3 minutes. Serve hot.

Pork with Green Pepper

PREPARATION TIME: 20 minutes

COOKING TIME: 1 hour 15 minutes

SERVES: 4 people

1lb pork fillet, cut into 2 inch strips

SEASONING
¼ tsp fine granulated sugar
¼ tsp monosodium glutamate (optional)
1¼ tsps light soy sauce
2 tsps sweet bean paste
2 tsps Shao Hsing wine or dry sherry
4 tbsps chicken broth

Oil for deep-frying
2 cloves garlic, peeled and cut into thin strips
1 green pepper, seeded and sliced into strips
1 green chili, sliced into strips
1 red chili, cut in half then sliced into strips

SAUCE
1 tsp cornstarch
1 tbsp water

Boil the pork in water for ¾ hour until cooked. Drain the pork and discard the water. Mix the seasoning ingredients together and stir in the pork. Leave to stand for 10 minutes. Heat the wok and add the oil for deep-frying. When oil is very hot fry the drained pork for a few minutes until golden brown. Remove and drain the pork and keep the oil for future use. Reheat the wok and add 1 tsp oil and stir-fry the garlic for 1 minute. Add the pepper and chilies

Right: Pork Chow Mein.

and stir-fry for 1 minute. Add the remaining seasoning mixture and the pork. Stir-fry over a gentle heat for 1-2 minutes and then add the blended sauce ingredients. Cook until the sauce thickens. Remove from the heat and serve immediately. Serve with mixed fried rice or rice noodles.

Pork with Plum Sauce

PREPARATION TIME: 40 minutes	
COOKING TIME: 30 minutes	
SERVES: 4 people	

1lb pork tenderloin, cut into 1″ cubes
1 tbsp cornstarch
1 tsp sesame oil
1 tbsp light soy sauce
1 tbsp sherry
1 tbsp brown sugar
½ tsp cinnamon
1 clove garlic, crushed
1 green onion, sliced finely
2 tbsps peanut oil
4 tbsps bottled plum sauce
¼ cup water
Salt
Pepper

GARNISH
Green onion flowers

Mix together cornstarch, sesame oil, light soy sauce, sherry, brown sugar, cinnamon and salt. Pour over pork, and toss together. Leave for at least 30 minutes. Remove pork and reserve marinade. Heat wok and add peanut oil. Add pork, and stir-fry until golden brown all over. Add green onion, plum sauce and water to wok, and mix together well. Bring to boil, cover, and simmer gently for 15 minutes, or until pork is tender, stirring occasionally. Add marinade, and bring to boil. Simmer gently for a further 5 minutes. Garnish with green onion flowers. (To make these, cut green onion into 2″ lengths. Carefully cut lengths into fine shreds, keeping one end intact, and then soak in cold water until curling.) Serve hot with boiled rice.

This page: Pork with Plum Sauce. Facing page: Beef with Green Beans (page 98) (top), Beef Steak with Ginger (page 88) (center right) and Sweet and Sour Beef (page 103) (bottom).

Pork Chop Suey

PREPARATION TIME: 35 minutes	
COOKING TIME: 10 minutes	
SERVES: 3-4 people	

MARINADE
1 tbsp water
½ tsp baking soda
2½ tsps dark soy sauce

½lb pork fillet, sliced into 2 inch pieces
3 tbsps cooked oil or cooking oil
1 onion, peeled and cut into pieces
1 clove of garlic, peeled and sliced
⅓ cup bamboo shoots, sliced
2 cups bean sprouts

SEASONING
Pinch salt
Pinch freshly ground black pepper
Pinch monosodium glutamate (optional)
3 tbsps light soy sauce
1 tsp fine granulated sugar
1 tsp cornstarch

SAUCE
1 tsp cornstarch
1 tbsp water

Mix the marinade ingredients together. Add the pork and leave for 15 minutes to marinate. Drain the pork and discard the marinade. Heat the oil in the wok and stir-fry pork for 2-3 minutes. Remove the pork. Add the onion, garlic and bamboo shoots to the wok and stir-fry for 1-2 minutes. Add the bean sprouts and stir-fry for 2 minutes. Remove onto a dish and add the mixed seasoning ingredients. Leave for 10 minutes. Return the pork and the vegetables to the wok. Add the blended sauce ingredients. Bring to the boil gently, stirring until the sauce thickens. Serve immediately.

Lamb Meatballs with Yogurt

PREPARATION TIME: 15 minutes	
COOKING TIME: 30 minutes	
SERVES: 4 people	

1lb lean ground lamb
2 cloves garlic, crushed
1 small onion, peeled and grated
½ tsp chili powder
1 tsp garam masala
1 tbsp chopped mint
2 tbsps breadcrumbs
1 egg, lightly beaten
2 tbsps oil
½ cup plain yogurt
Small pinch of saffron strands, or ¼ tsp ground turmeric
2 tbsps boiling water
Salt
Pepper

GARNISH
Fresh coriander or mint

In a bowl, mix together ground lamb, garlic, onion, chili powder, garam masala, mint and breadcrumbs. Add lightly beaten egg to bind ingredients together. Add salt and pepper to taste. Wet hands. Take a teaspoon of mixture, and roll between palms, forming small balls. Heat wok and add oil. Add meatballs, shake wok to make meatballs roll around, and fry until browned well all over. Add saffron or turmeric to 2 tbsps boiling water. Leave for 5 minutes. Add water to yogurt, and stir in until evenly mixed. Reheat meatballs and serve on yogurt. Garnish with mint or fresh coriander. Serve with rice.

Pork with Black Bean Sauce

PREPARATION TIME: 40 minutes	
COOKING TIME: 45 minutes	
SERVES: 4 people	

8oz lean pork, cut into 1" cubes
1 tbsp oil
1 red pepper, cored, seeds removed, and sliced

SAUCE
3 tbsps black beans, rinsed in cold water and crushed with back of a spoon
2 tbsps Chinese wine, or dry sherry
1 tsp grated ginger
2 tbsps light soy sauce
3 cloves garlic, crushed
1 tbsp cornstarch
⅔ cup water

Mix together black beans, wine, ginger, soy sauce and garlic. Blend cornstarch with 2 tbsps of water and add to mixture. Place pork in a bowl, and pour over sauce. Toss together well. Leave for at least 30 minutes. Heat wok, add oil and stir-fry red pepper for 3 minutes. Remove and set aside. Add pork, reserving marinade sauce. Stir-fry pork until browned well all over. Add marinade sauce and remaining water. Bring to the boil. Reduce heat, cover, and gently simmer for about 30 minutes, until pork is tender, stirring occasionally. Add more water if necessary. Just before serving, add red pepper and heat through. Serve with plain white rice.

Beef Steak with Ginger

PREPARATION TIME: 20-25 minutes	
COOKING TIME: 10-12 minutes	
SERVES: 2-3 people	

SEASONING
½ tsp baking soda
3 tbsps light soy sauce
2 tbsps rice wine or dry sherry
½ tsp salt
½ tsp ground black pepper

½ tsp fresh root ginger, peeled and minced
½lb beef fillet, sliced into 1 inch pieces

SAUCE
1 tsp fine granulated sugar
¼ tsp monosodium glutamate (optional)
1¼ tbsps dark soy sauce
3½ tbsps broth
Few drops sesame oil
1 tsp Shao Hsing wine

4 tbsps salad or olive oil
1 inch fresh root ginger, peeled and thinly sliced
4 green onions, chopped
½ cup bamboo shoots, thinly sliced
2 green chilies, sliced

Facing page: Lamb Meatballs with Yogurt (top) and Pork with Black Bean Sauce (bottom).

Mix the seasoning ingredients with the minced ginger. Add the beef and marinate for 20 minutes. Drain the beef and discard the marinade. Mix the sauce ingredients together. Heat 3 tbsps oil in the wok and fry the sliced ginger and onions for 2 minutes. Add the bamboo shoots and chilies and stir-fry for 1-2 minutes. Remove to a plate. Add the remaining oil to the wok and fry the beef for 2-3 minutes. Add the fried vegetables and stir-fry for 2 minutes. Add the well-stirred sauce ingredients and simmer gently until the mixture thickens. Simmer for another 1-2 minutes. Remove from heat and serve.

Sweet and Sour Pork with Peppers

PREPARATION TIME:
1 hour 15 minutes

COOKING TIME: 30 minutes

SERVES: 4 people

1lb pork tenderloin, cut into 1" cubes
1 large green pepper, cored, seeds removed, and chopped roughly
1 large yellow or red pepper, cored, seeds removed, and chopped roughly
1 small can or jar of Chinese mixed pickle
1 large onion, peeled and chopped finely
1¼ cups peanut oil

BATTER
1 egg
1 tsp peanut oil
¼ cup cornstarch
¼ cup flour
¼ tsp baking powder
Water

MARINADE
1 tbsp peanut oil
½ tsp light soy sauce
2 tsps Chinese wine, or 1 tbsp dry sherry
1 tsp cornstarch
1 tsp sugar
Pinch of salt
Pinch of pepper

SAUCE
¼ cup sugar
⅓ cup wine vinegar
⅓ cup water
1 tbsp tomato paste
Pinch of salt
1 tsp cornstarch
Few drops of red food coloring (if desired)

Mix together marinade ingredients. Pour over pork pieces and leave for about 1 hour, turning occasionally. Mix together batter ingredients, with enough water to form batter. Add pork. Heat peanut oil in wok. When hot, deep-fry pork pieces in small batches, so that they do not stick together. Remove when golden brown, using a slotted spoon, and set aside. Continue until all battered pork pieces are cooked. Heat oil again and repeat process, cooking pork for 5 minutes to make batter nice and crisp. Keep warm. Carefully drain off all but 1 tbsp of oil. Heat, and add onion, peppers and Chinese mixed pickle. Cover and cook for 3 minutes. Remove and set aside. Heat vinegar, water, sugar, tomato paste, red food coloring and salt. Slake cornstarch with 1 tbsp of water. Stir into sauce. Bring to the boil and cook for 3 minutes. Add pork and vegetables to sauce. Serve hot with rice.

Beef Worcestershire (top right) and Sweet and Sour Pork with Peppers (bottom right).

Beef Worcestershire

PREPARATION TIME: 40 minutes

COOKING TIME: 20 minutes

SERVES: 4 people

1lb sirloin or butt steak, cut into 1½" cubes
2oz wonton wrappers
⅔ cup oil for deep frying

SAUCE
2 tbsps Worcestershire sauce
1 tbsp dark soy sauce
1 tbsp sugar
Pinch of salt
Pinch of pepper
½ tsp cornstarch

Mix together ingredients for sauce, and pour over steak. Toss well. Leave for at least 30 minutes, turning occasionally. Meanwhile, heat oil in wok. Fold wonton wrappers in half diagonally and seal open corners with water and press together. Deep fry a few wonton wrappers at a time until golden brown. Remove with a slotted spoon and drain on paper towels. Repeat until there are enough wonton wrappers to go around the edge of the serving dish. Carefully remove all but 2 tbsps of oil from wok. Remove steak from sauce mixture and reserve. Heat wok, and when oil is hot, add steak and stir-fry until well browned. Pour over sauce and bring to the boil. Reduce heat and simmer, stirring continuously. When sauce thickens, and will coat steak well, place in warm serving dish and garnish with wonton wrappers. Serve immediately with boiled rice.

Beef with Green Pepper, Tomato and Black Beans

PREPARATION TIME: 30 minutes

MICROWAVE COOKING TIME: 8-10 minutes

SERVES: 4 people

1lb rump steak, cut in thin slices
4 tbsps soy sauce
2 tsps dry sherry or rice wine

SAUCE
3 tbsps salted black beans
2 tbsps water
1 cup brown stock
1 tbsp sugar
3 tbsps cornstarch dissolved in the stock
1 clove garlic, finely minced
1 large green pepper, cut in 1 inch pieces
3 tomatoes, peeled and quartered
Salt and pepper

Mix the steak, soy sauce and wine and leave to marinate, covered, in the refrigerator for 30 minutes. Crush the black beans and mix with the water. Leave to stand until ready to use. Combine all the ingredients in a shallow dish, except for the pepper

This page: Beef with Green Pepper, Tomato and Black Beans. Facing page: Pork Chops, Shanghai Style (top) and Lion's Head (page 94) (bottom).

and tomatoes. Cover the dish and cook on HIGH for 7-9 minutes, stirring halfway through the cooking time. Once the sauce has cleared, add the pepper and tomatoes and cook 1 minute further on HIGH. Serve with rice. Garnish with green onion brushes if desired.

Pork Chops, Shanghai Style

PREPARATION TIME: 15 minutes

MICROWAVE COOKING TIME: 14 minutes

SERVES: 4 people

⅓ cup soy sauce
1 tbsp brown sugar
1 tbsp oil
8 thin pork chops
1 onion, thinly sliced
2 tsps cornstarch mixed with 2 tsps water

Mix the soy sauce and sugar with ½

cup water. Heat a browning dish 5 minutes on HIGH. Pour in the oil and brown the pork on both sides about 2 minutes on HIGH. Brown in two batches if necessary. Remove the pork and add the onions. Cook to brown and soften slightly. Remove the onions from the browning dish and set aside. Return the pork chops to the dish and pour over the soy sauce mixture. Cover and cook a further 5 minutes on HIGH, or until the pork is tender. Remove the pork and keep warm. Mix the cornstarch and water with the soy sauce mixture. Stir well and cook 1 minute on HIGH to thicken slightly. Add the onions and cook a further 1 minute on HIGH. Pour over the pork to serve. Serve with stir-fried vegetables. Garnish with Chinese parsley leaves if desired.

Pork with Chili

PREPARATION TIME: 1 hour

COOKING TIME: 20 minutes

SERVES: 4 people

10oz pork tenderloin, cut into 1" cubes
1 green pepper, cored, seeds removed, and sliced
1 red chili pepper, seeds removed, and sliced finely
4 green onions, chopped
1 clove garlic, crushed
1 tsp sugar
1 tsp cornstarch
1 tsp peanut oil
1 tsp Chinese wine, or dry sherry
⅔ cup peanut oil, for deep frying

SAUCE
1 tsp chili powder
2 tbsps dark soy sauce
1 tsp Worcestershire sauce
½ tsp five-spice powder
Pinch of salt

Mix together garlic, sugar, 1 tsp peanut oil, wine and cornstarch, and pour over pork. Cover and leave for at least 1 hour, turning occasionally. Meanwhile, combine ingredients for sauce in a bowl. Mix well. Set aside. Heat oil in wok until hot. Toss in pork cubes, and cook until golden brown and cooked through – about 10 minutes. Drain and set aside. Carefully remove all but 1 tbsp of oil from wok. Heat oil and add green pepper, chili pepper and green onions. Stir-fry for 2 minutes. Add sauce and pork, and bring to boil, stirring continuously. Adjust seasoning. Serve immediately with rice or noodles.

Happys' Curry

PREPARATION TIME: 20 minutes

COOKING TIME: 30 minutes

SERVES: 4 people

1lb skirt or butt steak, cut into 1" cubes
8oz potatoes, peeled and diced
2 onions, peeled and chopped very finely
3 cloves garlic, crushed
1 tsp grated ginger root
1 tsp ground turmeric
½ tsp chili powder
1 tsp garam masala
½ tsp salt
1¼ cups water
¼ cup peanut oil

GARNISH
Fresh coriander

Heat wok and add oil. Add ginger, garlic and onion, and fry gently for 5 minutes. Add turmeric, chili powder, garam masala and salt, and fry for 30 seconds. Add steak, and stir-fry until browned well all over. Add potatoes and water, and bring to the boil. Reduce heat, and cover. Simmer gently until meat is tender and potatoes are cooked. Garnish with fresh coriander and serve with rice if desired.

Lion's Head

PREPARATION TIME: 20 minutes

MICROWAVE COOKING TIME: 19-20 minutes

SERVES: 4-6 people

2lbs ground pork
⅓ cup soy sauce
2 tsps dry sherry
1 tsp brown sugar
¼ cup cornstarch
2 tbsps oil
1 tsp granulated sugar
1½ tbsps soy sauce
1 head Chinese cabbage
Salt (if necessary)

Pork with Chili (right) and Happys' Curry (below).

½ red chili pepper, finely chopped
4 tbsps soy sauce
½ cup stock
2 tbsps white wine
1 tsp vinegar
1 tsp sugar
1 tbsp cornstarch
1 small red pepper, cut in small dice
1 small green pepper, cut in small dice
4 green onions, sliced
½ cup roasted peanuts
Dash sesame oil

Heat a browning dish for 5 minutes on HIGH. Combine oil and lamb and add to the dish. Cook for about 2 minutes, turning often. Cook in two batches if necessary. Add the garlic, ginger and chili pepper and cook a further 2 minutes on HIGH. Mix the soy sauce, stock, wine, vinegar, sugar and cornstarch together and add to the meat. Cover the browning dish or transfer the ingredients to a covered casserole dish. Cook on MEDIUM a further 4-6 minutes or until the lamb is tender. Add the diced peppers and cook a further 1 minute on HIGH. Stir in the sesame oil, peanuts and the green onions. Heat 30 seconds on HIGH. Serve with rice.

Shredded Pork with Preserved Vegetables

PREPARATION TIME: 30 minutes
COOKING TIME: 6-8 minutes
SERVES: 3 people

Pinch monosodium glutamate (optional)
2 tsps cornstarch
Salt and freshly ground black pepper to taste
½lb lean pork, shredded
Oil for deep-frying
1 inch fresh root ginger, peeled and shredded
½ cup shelled green peas, lightly cooked
½ tsp fine granulated sugar
2 tsps Shao Hsing wine or dry sherry
8oz mixed Shanghai preserved vegetables, in brine
1 tsp sesame oil

Mix the monosodium glutamate, cornstarch and a pinch of salt. Add the

Mix pork, ⅓ cup soy sauce, sherry, brown sugar, 1 tbsp cornstarch and shape into 2 inch balls. Heat a browning dish 5 minutes on HIGH. Add the oil and the pork balls. Brown the pork balls 3-5 minutes on HIGH, turning often. Cook in 2 batches, re-heating the dish in between each batch. If the browning dish has a cover, leave the pork balls in it or transfer to a large casserole. Add the granulated sugar, remaining soy sauce and 1 cup water. Cover and cook 9 minutes on HIGH. Turn the pork balls often and rearrange to bring those in the middle of the dish to the outside. Shred the Chinese cabbage finely and add it to the casserole with the pork balls. Cook 1 minute on HIGH. Remove the pork and Chinese cabbage to a serving dish and keep warm. Mix the

remaining cornstarch with 2 tbsps water and add to the cooking liquid from the pork balls. Cook 2-3 minutes, uncovered, on HIGH or until the sauce has thickened. Arrange the cabbage on a serving dish with the pork balls on top. Pour over the sauce to serve.

Kung-Pao Lamb

PREPARATION TIME: 20 minutes
MICROWAVE COOKING TIME: 10½-11½ minutes
SERVES: 4 people

1lb lamb fillet or meat from the leg, thinly sliced
2 tbsps oil
1 clove garlic, finely minced
1 small piece fresh ginger root, grated

Facing page: Kung Pao Lamb. This page: Sweet and Sour Pork (top), Diced Pork with Walnuts (page 108) (center) and Shredded Pork with Preserved Vegetables (bottom).

sprinkle with the sugar, wine and salt and pepper to taste. Stir-fry for another minute and add the well-drained preserved vegetables. Allow to heat through and then stir gently. Sprinkle on the sesame oil and serve. Serve as a side dish or on a bed of plain fried noodles.

Sweet and Sour Pork

PREPARATION TIME: 20 minutes, plus 20 minutes to marinate

COOKING TIME: 15-20 minutes

SERVES: 4 people

BATTER
3 tbsps all-purpose flour
1 tbsp cornstarch
1½ tsps baking soda
2 tbsps salad or olive oil

12oz lean pork, cut into 1 inch cubes

SEASONING
1 tsp fine granulated sugar
1 tsp salt
2½ tbsps light soy sauce
1½ tsps dark soy sauce
1 tbsp cooked oil
1 tbsp water
Cornstarch
Oil for deep-frying
2 cloves garlic, cut into thin strips
1 large onion, peeled and cut into ½ inch pieces
1 carrot, sliced into ⅛x1x2 inch thin pieces
Pinch salt

SWEET AND SOUR SAUCE
3 tbsps brown sugar
1 tbsp ketchup
1 cup chicken broth or water
4 tbsps wine-flavored vinegar
1½ tsps light soy sauce
Few slices fresh root ginger, peeled
1 tbsp cornstarch
Few drops of red food coloring
2 tsps cooked oil

pork and let it stand for 15 minutes. Heat the oil in a wok and deep-fry the pork for 3 minutes. Remove the pork and drain. Reserve oil for future use. Reheat wok and add 2 tsps deep-fried oil. Stir-fry the ginger and green peas for 1 minute. Add the pork and

Mix the batter ingredients together, adding sufficient water to make a thick coating batter. Wash and drain the pork. Mix with the seasoning ingredients and marinate for 15-20 minutes. Drain the pork and discard the marinade. Roll the pork cubes in cornstarch. Heat the oil for deep-frying.

Dip the pork cubes in batter and fry in the hot oil until golden brown. Fry a few at a time until all the pork has been fried. Drain well and keep warm in a low oven. Heat wok and add 2 tsps deep-fried oil. Stir-fry the garlic, onions and carrots for 3-4 minutes. Season with salt and fry for a further minute. Mix the sweet and sour sauce ingredients together and add to the wok. Stir the mixture until it thickens. Pour over the fried pork cubes and serve immediately. Note: sliced green peppers can also be added along with the carrots and onions.

Beef with Green Beans

PREPARATION TIME: 30 minutes
COOKING TIME: 12 minutes
SERVES: 4 people

SEASONING
½ tsp baking soda
1 tsp cornstarch
1¼ tbsps light soy sauce
2 tbsps water
1 tsp cooked oil

1lb lean beef, thinly sliced into 1 inch pieces

SAUCE
¼ tsp salt
1 tsp monosodium glutamate (optional)
1½ tsps light soy sauce
1½ tsps dark soy sauce
1 tsp Shao Hsing wine (optional)
½ cup broth
2 tsps cornstarch

3 tbsps salad or olive oil
2 cloves of garlic, peeled and sliced
1 onion, peeled and cut into wedges
1 inch fresh root ginger, peeled and thinly sliced
6oz Chinese long beans, cut into 3 inch pieces (or whole tender green beans)
Salt and freshly ground black pepper to taste

Mix seasoning ingredients together. Add the beef and marinate for 20 minutes. Drain the meat and discard the marinade. Mix the sauce ingredients together. Heat 2 tbsps oil in the wok until it smokes. Reduce the heat and add the garlic and the beef and stir-fry for 3-4 minutes. Remove the meat and keep on one side. Add the remaining oil to the wok and add the

onion, ginger and long beans and stir-fry for 2-3 minutes. Add the fried beef. Cover and fry for a further 1 minute. Stir in the sauce ingredients and bring to the boil. Simmer gently for 2-3 minutes. Season with salt and pepper. Remove from heat and serve.

Spiced Liver

PREPARATION TIME: 10 minutes
COOKING TIME: 20 minutes
SERVES: 4 people

1lb lamb's liver, cut into 1 inch cubes
½ cup soy sauce
3-4 green onions, chopped
2¼ tbsps rice wine or dry sherry
2 tsps fine granulated sugar
1 inch fresh root ginger, peeled and finely chopped
½ tsp freshly ground black pepper
Pinch anise powder

Boil the liver in sufficient water to just cover, for 3-4 minutes. Drain well. Add soy sauce, green onions, wine, sugar, ginger, pepper and anise powder. Simmer gently for 10-15 minutes, covered, until the liver is tender. Serve as a side dish.

Braised Hong Kong Beef

PREPARATION TIME: 30 minutes
COOKING TIME: about 15-17 minutes
SERVES: 4 people

2 tbsps salad or olive oil
1lb fillet of beef, sliced into matchstick size strips
1 onion, peeled and sliced
1 inch fresh root ginger, peeled and cut into thin strips
3-4 fresh tomatoes, cut into thin wedges
½lb carrots, scraped and cut into 2 inch sticks
2½ tsps brown sugar
½ tsp five spice powder
2¼ tbsps light soy sauce
1 tbsp rice wine or dry sherry
2 tbsps water
Salt to taste

Heat the oil in a wok and fry the beef for 3-4 minutes. Add the onion, ginger, tomatoes and carrots. Stir-fry for 2-3 minutes. Add the sugar, five spice powder, soy sauce, wine and water.

Spiced Liver (top) and Braised Hong Kong Beef (right).

DEVILLING MIXTURE
1 tsp salt
1 tsp sugar
½ tsp ground black pepper
½ tsp ground ginger
½ tsp dry mustard
¼ tsp curry powder

GARNISH
Sprig of parsley

Skin the kidneys and cut in half lengthwise. Mix the dry devilling mixture together, and coat kidneys well. Leave for at least 1 hour. Heat wok and melt butter. Brown the kidneys quickly in the hot butter. Add Worcestershire sauce and soy sauce, and bring to the boil. Cover and simmer for 15 minutes thickening with cornstarch mixed with water if necessary. Garnish with parsley and serve with saffron rice.

Calves' Liver with Piquant Sauce

PREPARATION TIME: 10 minutes

COOKING TIME: 25 minutes

SERVES: 4 people

1lb calves' liver
1 onion, peeled and sliced
1 tbsp oil
2 tbsps butter
1 tbsp flour
1¼ cups brown stock, or 1¼ cups hot water and 1 beef bouillon cube
2 tbsps tomato, mango, or other fruit relish
1 tbsp tomato paste
1 clove garlic, crushed
1 tsp dry mustard, mixed with 2 tsps water
Salt
Pepper

GARNISH
Chopped parsley

Heat wok and add butter. When melted, stir in flour and cook until lightly browned. Remove from heat

Season with salt to taste and cook gently for 8-10 minutes. Serve as a side dish.

Devilled Kidneys

PREPARATION TIME:
1 hour 15 minutes

COOKING TIME: 20 minutes

SERVES: 4 people

1lb veal kidneys
1 tbsp Worcestershire sauce
1 tbsp dark soy sauce
2 tbsps butter
1 tsp cornstarch
1 tbsp water

This page: Devilled Kidneys (top) and Calves' Liver with Piquant Sauce (bottom). Facing page: Kidneys with Bacon (page 106) (top) and Piquant Lambs' Livers (page 108) (bottom).

and gradually stir in stock. Return to heat and add tomato paste and garlic. Stir until boiling. Add mustard and salt and pepper to taste, and let simmer for 5 minutes. Add relish and mix well. Remove from wok and set aside. Meanwhile, slice liver very thinly. Wash and drain on paper towels. Heat wok and add oil. When hot add onion. Fry gently over medium heat until just turning color. Add slices of liver in a single layer, and fry for about 3 minutes on each side, depending on thickness of slices. The liver should be cooked through and still tender. Do not overcook. Add piquant sauce to wok and toss together. Sprinkle with chopped parsley. Serve immediately on boiled rice.

Steamed Lamb with Mushroom Sauce

PREPARATION TIME: 20-25 minutes
COOKING TIME: 2 hours 10 minutes
SERVES: 6 people

2¼lb boned leg of lamb, cut into 1 inch cubes
2 onions, thinly sliced

Salt and freshly ground black pepper
2 tsps salad or olive oil
2 cloves of garlic, peeled and sliced
1 tsp cornstarch
Pinch monosodium glutamate (optional)
6 tbsps light soy sauce
3½ tbsps rice wine or dry sherry
1 tsp crushed black pepper
1 inch fresh root ginger, peeled and thinly sliced
Few drops sesame oil

Put the lamb into a saucepan and add sufficient water to cover. Boil for 5 minutes. Drain the lamb and retain the water. Arrange the lamb cubes in a deep dish and sprinkle the onions on top. Season with pepper and salt. Heat the oil in a wok and fry the garlic until brown. Remove the garlic and discard. Mix together the cornstarch, monosodium glutamate, soy sauce, wine, crushed pepper, ginger and 4 tbsps reserved lamb broth. Stir the cornstarch mixture into the oil in the wok and cook for 1-2 minutes. Pour over the lamb. Cover the lamb with overlapping foil and tie around the rim. Put the dish in a steamer and steam over boiling water for 2 hours. Serve with the sesame oil sprinkled over the lamb.

Lamb with Tomatoes

PREPARATION TIME: 20 minutes
COOKING TIME: about 10 minutes
SERVES: 2 people

2 tsps cornstarch
½ tsp salt
1½ tbsps light soy sauce
4½ tbsps water
3 tbsps salad or olive oil
½ inch fresh root ginger, sliced
8oz lamb fillet, cut across the grain in thin strips of ½x2 inch
2 green onions, chopped
1 onion, peeled and cut into 1 inch pieces
1 green pepper, seeded and cut into strips
1 tsp five spice powder
3-4 small, firm tomatoes, cut into ½ inch pieces

Mix the cornstarch, salt, soy sauce, water and 1 tsp of the oil together. Keep on one side. Heat the remaining oil in a wok and fry the ginger and lamb for 2-3 minutes. Add the onions, green pepper and curry powder and stir-fry for 3-4 minutes. Stir in the cornstarch mixture and cook for 1 minute. Add the tomatoes and cook until the sauce thickens. Serve as a side dish.

Mongolian Lamb with Onions

PREPARATION TIME: 20 minutes
COOKING TIME: 8-10 minutes
SERVES: 4 people

1lb lean, boned lamb, cut into ¼x2 inch strips
1 egg white
2 cloves of garlic, sliced
½ tsp five spice powder
½ inch fresh root ginger, peeled and thinly sliced
1 tbsp cornstarch
1¼ tbsps light soy sauce
3½ tbsps rice wine or dry sherry
2 tbsps water
3 tbsps cooked oil
6 green onions, chopped

Mix the lamb with the egg white, garlic, five spice powder, ginger root and 1 tsp cornstarch and 1 tsp soy sauce. Keep on one side. Mix the remaining cornstarch, soy sauce, wine and water together. Heat the wok and add the oil. When it begins to smoke, add the beef mixture. Reduce the heat and stir-fry for 3-4 minutes until the meat browns slightly. Remove and keep on one side. Add the onions and the cornstarch, soy sauce and wine mixture to the wok. Stir until it thickens. Return the meat to the wok and simmer gently for 3-4 minutes, or until the meat is tender. Serve as a main dish.

Sweet and Sour Beef

PREPARATION TIME: 15 minutes
COOKING TIME: 15 minutes
SERVES: 4 people

BATTER
A generous ½ cup all-purpose flour
1½ tsps baking powder
4 tbsps cornstarch
1 tbsp salad or olive oil

3 tbsps salad or olive oil
8oz fillet of beef, cut into 1 inch cubes
1 onion, peeled and cut into wedges
1 inch fresh root ginger, peeled and thinly sliced
1 clove garlic, peeled and thinly sliced
1 green pepper, seeded and chopped

SWEET AND SOUR SAUCE
4 tbsps brown sugar
¼ tsp salt
4 tbsps wine-flavored vinegar
1 tsp fresh root ginger, peeled and minced
⅓ cup water
1 tbsp cornstarch
2 tsps cooked oil
Few drops food coloring
Oil for deep frying

Lamb with Tomatoes (far left), Steamed Lamb with Mushroom Sauce (left) and Mongolian Lamb with Onions (below).

Steak with Peanut Sauce

PREPARATION TIME: 45 minutes	
COOKING TIME: 30 minutes	
SERVES: 4 people	

1lb sirloin or butt steak, cut into ½" cubes
1 tbsp oil

MARINADE
½ tsp chili powder
Juice of half a lemon
2 tsps brown sugar
½ tsp salt
1 tsp ground coriander
1 tsp ground cumin

PEANUT SAUCE
2 tbsps peanut oil
⅔ cup raw shelled peanuts
2 red chili peppers, seeds removed, and
    chopped (or 1 tsp chili powder)
2 shallots, chopped
1 clove garlic, crushed
1 tsp brown sugar
Juice of half a lemon
Salt

Mix together marinade ingredients, and marinate steak for at least 30 minutes. Make sauce. Heat wok, add half peanut oil and heat gently. Stir-fry peanuts for 2-3 minutes. Remove from wok, and drain on paper towels. Crush chili peppers, shallots and garlic to a smooth paste or blend. Grind peanuts to fine powder. Heat remaining oil in wok over a medium heat. Fry chili paste for 1-2 minutes. Add ⅔ cup water. Bring to the boil. Add peanuts, brown sugar, lemon juice and salt to taste. Stir until sauce is thick – approximately 10 minutes. Put in bowl, and keep warm. Heat wok, and add oil. Stir-fry meat until well browned all over. Serve with peanut sauce and boiled rice.

Steak with Black Bean Sauce

PREPARATION TIME: 1 hour 15 minutes	
COOKING TIME: 20 minutes	
SERVES: 4 people	

For the batter: sift the flour, baking powder and cornstarch. Beat in the oil and add sufficient water to make a thick, smooth batter. Heat the 3 tbsps oil in a wok and stir-fry the beef for 2 minutes. Remove the beef. Fry the onion, ginger, garlic and green pepper for 2-3 minutes in the same oil. Remove the wok from the heat. Mix the sauce ingredients together and add to the wok. Return the wok to the heat and bring to the boil gently. Lower the heat and simmmer gently for 2-3 minutes until thick and clear. Meanwhile, dip the beef cubes into the batter and deep fry in hot oil until golden brown and crisp. Drain on absorbent paper. Arrange in a deep dish and pour the hot sauce over the beef. Serve with a chow mein dish or fried rice. Thinly sliced carrots, cucumber and zucchini may also be added along with the onion, ginger and green pepper.

Put sliced steak into a bowl, and sprinkle over baking soda. Add 1 tbsp of light soy sauce, 1 tsp of sugar, wine, sesame oil, salt and pepper, and leave to marinate for at least 1 hour. Heat wok and add 2 tbsps peanut oil. When hot, add steak and fry quickly. Remove from heat, and remove steak. Set aside. Add onion, green pepper, bamboo shoots, and a pinch of salt to wok. Cover and cook for 3 minutes. Remove and set aside. Make black bean sauce by crushing black beans and mixing with garlic, ginger, 1 tsp of sugar and 1 tbsp of peanut oil. Heat wok, add 1 tbsp of oil and pour in black bean mixture. Add steak and vegetables and mix well. Make seasoning sauce by mixing cornstarch with remaining 1 tbsp of light soy sauce, and adding 1 tsp of sugar. When well mixed, pour into wok and stir. Bring to the boil and cook for 3 minutes. Serve hot with rice.

Braised Pork with Spinach and Mushrooms

PREPARATION TIME:	20 minutes
COOKING TIME:	30 minutes
SERVES:	4 people

1lb pork tenderloin, cut into thin strips
8oz spinach leaves, washed, hard stalks
*   removed, and shredded*
4 dried Chinese mushrooms, soaked in
*   hot water for 20 minutes, stems*
*   discarded, and caps sliced finely*
½ tsp ground nutmeg
2 tbsps water
2 tbsps peanut oil
1 onion, peeled and quartered
1 clove garlic, crushed
1 tbsp flour
Salt
Pepper

Heat wok, add 1 tsp of oil, and roll it around to coat the surface. Put nutmeg and spinach in wok, and cook gently for 5 minutes. Remove from pan. Add remaining oil to wok and fry garlic and onion over gentle heat for 5 minutes. Remove from wok. Meanwhile, add a good pinch of salt and freshly-ground black pepper

Facing page: Steak with Peanut Sauce (top) and Noodles with Pork and Shrimp (page 106) (bottom). This page: Braised Pork with Spinach and Mushrooms (top) and Steak with Black Bean Sauce (bottom).

8oz sirloin or butt steak, thinly sliced
1 large onion, peeled and chopped
1 large green pepper, cored, seeds removed,
*   and diced*
3 cloves garlic, crushed
1 tsp grated ginger root

1 small can sliced bamboo shoots, drained
3 tsps black beans
2 tbsps light soy sauce
4 tbsps peanut oil
1 tsp Chinese wine, or 2 tsps dry sherry
3 tsps sugar
1 tsp cornstarch
1 tsp sesame oil
Pinch of baking soda
Salt
Pepper

to the flour and toss in the pork, coating well. Fry pork until each piece is browned all over. Add water and mushrooms, and return onion mixture to wok. Cover and simmer gently for 10 minutes, stirring occasionally. Add spinach and salt and pepper to taste, and cook, uncovered, for 2 minutes. Serve hot with steamed rice.

Lamb with Cherries

PREPARATION TIME: 15 minutes

COOKING TIME: 1 hour 15 minutes

SERVES: 4 people

1lb boneless lamb from leg, cut into 1" cubes
2 tbsps butter or margarine
1 onion, peeled and chopped finely
½ tsp turmeric
½ tsp cinnamon
½ tsp ground nutmeg
1 tsp brown sugar
1 can black cherries, stoned
1 tbsp lemon juice
1 tbsp arrowroot or cornstarch
⅔ cup water
Salt
Pepper

Heat half butter in wok. Add lamb and fry quickly to brown well all over. Remove from wok and set aside. Add remaining butter and onion and fry for 2 minutes. Add turmeric, cinnamon, nutmeg and brown sugar, and fry for a further 1 minute. Add salt and pepper to taste. Return lamb to wok and add water. Cover and gently simmer for 45 minutes to 1 hour, until lamb is tender. Add undrained cherries. Blend arrowroot or cornstarch with lemon juice and stir into mixture. Bring to boil and simmer for 4 minutes or until sauce has thickened. Serve hot with rice.

Noodles with Pork and Shrimp

PREPARATION TIME: 20 minutes

COOKING TIME: 15 minutes

SERVES: 4 people

8oz fine egg noodles

¼ cup peanut oil
1 onion, peeled and chopped finely
4oz pork, finely sliced
4oz shrimp, shelled and de-veined
2 cloves garlic, crushed
1 tbsp light soy sauce
1 tsp sambal manis or sambal oelek
¼ cabbage, shredded
1 green chili pepper, seeds removed, and sliced
2 sticks celery, sliced
Salt
Pepper

GARNISH
Sliced cucumber
Sliced green onions

Soak noodles in hot water for 8 minutes, or boil until cooked. Rinse in cold water. Drain in a colander. Set aside. Heat wok and add oil. Stir-fry onion, garlic and chili until onion starts to color. Add sambal manis or sambal oelek. Add pork, celery, cabbage and salt and pepper, and stir-fry for 3 minutes. Add soy sauce, noodles and shrimp, and toss mixture to heat through well. Place in a warm serving dish, surrounded with sliced cucumber and sprinkled with green onions on top.

Kidneys with Bacon

PREPARATION TIME: 20 minutes

COOKING TIME: 25 minutes

SERVES: 4 people

1lb lambs' kidneys
1 tbsp tomato relish
8 rashers bacon, diced
1 onion, peeled and quartered
3 cloves garlic, crushed
2 tbsps oil
1 tbsp light soy sauce
1 tbsp cornstarch
3 tbsps sherry
1 tbsp chopped parsley
2 tbsps water
Salt
Pepper

GARNISH
Sprig of parsley

Cut kidneys in half and remove hard core with a sharp knife or scissors. Cut a lattice design on back of kidneys. Pour over sherry, and set aside for 15 minutes. Heat wok and

add oil. Add bacon, onion and garlic, and stir-fry for 5 minutes. Remove from wok. Add kidneys, reserving sherry, and fry for 3 minutes. Stir in tomato relish. Add soy sauce and water to wok, and return bacon and onion mixture. Add salt and pepper to taste. Cover and simmer gently for 10 minutes. Meanwhile, blend cornstarch with sherry marinade.

Add parsley and cornstarch mixture, and stir, cooking gently until sauce thickens. Garnish with parsley. Serve hot with rice.

Lamb with Cherries (left) and Five-Spice Beef with Broccoli (page 111) (bottom left).

Deep-Fried Pork Meatballs

PREPARATION TIME: 25 minutes

COOKING TIME: about 12 minutes

MAKES: 16 meatballs

1lb coarsely ground lean pork
1 small onion, finely chopped
1 green chili, chopped
Salt and freshly ground black pepper to
   taste
½ inch fresh root ginger, peeled and finely
   chopped
1 egg, beaten
1 tbsp cornstarch
2 tsps dark soy sauce
2 sprigs Chinese parsley, finely chopped
1 tsp cooked oil
Oil for deep frying
2 green onions, chopped (for garnishing)
1 green pepper, seeded and cut into rings
   (for garnishing) (optional)

Mix the ground pork with the chopped
onion, chili, salt and pepper to taste,
chopped ginger, beaten egg, cornstarch,
soy sauce, parsley and cooked oil.
Leave to stand for 10 minutes. Mould
into 16 even-sized balls. Heat the oil in
the wok for deep frying and slide a few
pork balls into the oil. Fry over a gentle
heat for 5-6 minutes until golden
brown and tender. Remove and drain
on kitchen paper. Fry all the meatballs
and serve with chopped green onions
and green pepper rings sprinkled on
top. Serve as a snack, as a starter or as
a side dish.

Bean Sprouts with Chopped Pork

PREPARATION TIME: 15 minutes

COOKING TIME: 10 minutes

SERVES: 4 people

2 cups ground lean pork

MARINADE
½ tsp salt
1¼ tbsps light soy sauce
1 egg white, beaten
1 tsp cornstarch

3 cups bean sprouts
Salad or olive oil for cooking

SEASONING
½ tsp salt
½ tsp fine granulated sugar
½ tsp monosodium glutamate (optional)
2 tsps soy sauce
1 tsp rice wine or dry sherry
1 tbsp oyster sauce

½ inch fresh root ginger, peeled and thinly
   sliced
2-3 green onions, chopped
½ cup chicken broth

SAUCE
½ tsp cornstarch
1 tbsp water or broth
Few drops of sesame oil

Mix the pork with the marinade
ingredients and keep on one side for 10
minutes. Trim the bean sprouts and
chop them coarsely. Heat 2 tbsps oil in
the wok. Stir-fry the bean sprouts for 1
minute to evaporate excess water and
moisture. Remove the bean sprouts
and keep on a plate. Mix the seasoning
ingredients together. Heat 3 tbsps oil in
the wok until it smokes. Stir-fry the
pork for 2 minutes and then add the
ginger, onions and bean sprouts. Stir-
fry for 2-3 minutes. Add the seasoning
ingredients and stir-fry for 1 minute.
Add the chicken broth and the
blended sauce ingredients. Cook until
the sauce thickens. Serve immediately.

Diced Pork with Walnuts

PREPARATION TIME: 30 minutes

COOKING TIME: 16-18 minutes

SERVES: 3 people

¾ cup shelled walnuts
Oil for deep-frying

SEASONING
1¾ tsps light soy sauce
Few drops sesame oil
Salt and freshly ground black pepper to
   taste
1 tbsp salad or olive oil
1 tbsp water
1 tbsp cornstarch
Pinch monosodium glutamate (optional)

½lb pork fillet, cut into cubes
1 carrot, thinly sliced

1 onion, peeled and cut into pieces
3 green onions, chopped
1 inch fresh root ginger, peeled and thinly
   sliced

SAUCE
⅓ cup broth
1 tsp cornstarch

Cook the walnuts in boiling water for
3-4 minutes. Drain the nuts thoroughly.
Deep-fry the walnuts until lightly
browned. Remove and drain. Use oil
for cooking. Mix the seasoning
ingredients together and add the pork.
Leave to marinate for 15 minutes.
Discard marinade. Heat 2 tbsps oil in
the wok and stir-fry the carrots for 2
minutes. Add the onions and root
ginger and stir-fry for 1 minute. Add 2
tsps of the sauce broth and remove to a
plate. Add the drained pork cubes and
1 tbsp oil to the wok and stir-fry for 4-5
minutes. Mix the remaining broth and
the cornstarch together for the sauce.
Return the walnuts and carrots to the
wok, together with the blended sauce
ingredients. Mix well and simmer until
the sauce thickens. Remove and serve
immediately. Serve with rice noodle or
fried rice.

Piquant Lambs' Livers

PREPARATION TIME: 15 minutes

COOKING TIME: 20 minutes

SERVES: 4 people

1lb lambs' livers, cut into thin strips
4 tbsps butter or margarine
2 tbsps wine vinegar
1 onion, peeled and sliced finely
⅓ cup white wine
1 tbsp chopped parsley
1 tbsp flour
Salt
Pepper

GARNISH
Chopped parsley

Combine flour with a good pinch of
salt and freshly-ground black pepper.

**Bean Sprouts with Chopped Pork (top
right) and Deep-Fried Pork Meatballs
(bottom).**

Toss in liver and coat well. Heat wok and add half the butter over gentle heat. Add onion and fry gently until transparent. Add vinegar and cook over high heat until vinegar has evaporated. Add remaining butter and when hot add liver. Stir-fry briskly for about 3 minutes. Add wine, parsley, and salt and pepper to taste. Bring to the boil and simmer for 5 minutes. Sprinkle with chopped parsley and serve with saffron rice.

Sesame Beef with Dates

PREPARATION TIME: 20 minutes, plus 30 minutes to marinate
COOKING TIME: 12-15 minutes
SERVES: 4 people

SEASONING A
½ tsp baking soda
1¼ tbsps light soy sauce
1 tbsp salad or olive oil
1¾ tsps cornstarch

1lb beef fillet, thinly sliced into 2 inch pieces
20 dried dates (red or dark), soaked and stoned

SEASONING B
1 tsp monosodium glutamate (optional)
1½ tsps brown sugar
2 tsps bean paste
A generous ¾ cup beef broth
Salt to taste

4 tbsps cooked oil, or plain oil
1 inch fresh root ginger, peeled and thinly sliced
2 green onions, sliced

SAUCE
1¼ tbsps cornstarch
2½ tbsps water or broth
2 tbsps sesame seeds

Mix the ingredients for seasoning A. Mix with the beef and marinate for 30 minutes. Drain meat and discard marinade. Drain soaked dates; slice most of them into 4 long pieces, leaving a few whole. Mix the dates with seasoning B. Heat oil in a wok and stir-fry beef for 4-5 minutes. Add ginger, green onions, dates and seasoning B

and gently bring to the boil. Add the blended sauce ingredients. Cover and simmer for 3-4 minutes over a gentle heat until the sauce thickens and becomes clear. Remove from the heat, place on a serving dish and keep warm. Heat a wok or skillet and add the sesame seeds. Dry-roast for 2 minutes until they begin to crackle and turn golden brown. Sprinkle over the beef and serve immediately.

Stir-Fried Beef with Onions

PREPARATION TIME: 30 minutes
COOKING TIME: 10 minutes
SERVES: 4 people

MARINADE
1 tbsp cornstarch
1 egg white
1 tbsp salad or olive oil
1 tsp baking soda

1lb beef fillet, cut into 1 inch strips

SEASONING
1 tsp Shao Hsing wine
1¼ tbsps light soy sauce
1 tsp dark soy sauce
½ tsp salt
½ tsp freshly ground black pepper
1 tsp monosodium glutamate (optional)

Oil for frying
1 small onion, peeled and thickly sliced
3 green onions, chopped lengthwise
2 leeks, white part only, cut into 1½ inch slices
1 tsp sesame oil

Mix the marinade ingredients with the beef strips. Leave to marinate for 20 minutes. Mix all the seasoning ingredients together in a small bowl. Heat 2 tbsps oil in a wok and when it is smoking, add the beef. Reduce the heat and stir-fry for 4-5 minutes. Remove the meat and keep the oil for future use. Heat the wok, add 2 tbsps fresh oil and stir-fry the onion and leeks for 2 minutes. Add seasoning mixture and beef and stir-fry for 1-2 minutes. Sprinkle sesame oil over the top and mix well. Serve immediately. Use as a main dish or a side dish.

Shredded Beef with Vegetables

PREPARATION TIME: 15 minutes
COOKING TIME: 10 minutes
SERVES: 2-3 people

8oz lean beef, cut into thin strips
Pinch salt
4 tbsps salad or olive oil
2 red and green chilies, cut in half then sliced into strips
1 tsp black vinegar
1 stem of celery, cut into 2 inch thin strips
2 carrots, cut into 2 inch thin strips
1 leek, white part only, sliced into 2 inch thin strips
2 cloves, garlic, peeled and finely chopped

SEASONING
1 tsp light soy sauce
1 tsp dark soy sauce
2 tsps Shao Hsing wine
1 tsp fine granulated sugar
Pinch monosodium glutamate (optional)
½ tsp freshly ground black pepper

Put the beef into a bowl and sprinkle with salt; rub salt into meat. Heat 1½ tsps oil in a wok until it begins to smoke. Reduce heat and add beef and chilies and stir-fry for 4-5 minutes. Add remaining oil and stir-fry beef until it turns crispy. Add vinegar and mix until it evaporates, then add celery, carrots, leeks and garlic. Stir-fry for 2 minutes. Mix the seasoning ingredients and pour over the beef and cook for 2 minutes. Serve immediately.

Szechuan Beef

PREPARATION TIME: 20 minutes
MICROWAVE COOKING TIME: 6-18 minutes
SERVES: 4 people

1lb rump steak, shredded
2 tbsp oil
½ dried chili pepper, crushed
4 tbsps soy sauce
½ cup stock
2 tbsps cornstarch
3 sticks celery, shredded
1 sweet red pepper, shredded

Cut steak into thin slices, then into narrow strips. Mix together with garlic, ginger, and five-spice powder. Heat wok, add 15ml (1 tbsp) of oil, and stir-fry broccoli for 8 minutes. Remove broccoli and add remaining oil. Add meat, and stir-fry for 3 minutes. Add broccoli, soy sauce, salt and water, and heat to simmering point. Mix cornstarch with cold water, and pour into wok, stirring continuously until liquid thickens. Toss in chives, stir, and serve immediately with boiled rice.

Guy's Curry (Hot)

PREPARATION TIME: 40 minutes

COOKING TIME:
2 hours 15 minutes

SERVES: 4 people

2lbs steak, skirt or rump, cut into
    ½" cubes
1½ cups coconut cream
1 onion, peeled and finely chopped
3 cloves garlic, chopped
2 tbsps golden raisins
1 tbsp curry leaves
1 dsp cumin
1 dsp coriander
1 tbsp vindaloo curry paste or powder (or
    milder if a curry less hot than vindaloo
    is desired)
1 carrot, grated
2 apples, chopped finely
1 banana, sliced finely
2 tomatoes, chopped finely
1 red pepper, cored, seeds removed, and
    chopped finely
6 small pieces lemon rind
2 tbsps desiccated coconut
2 tsps sugar
1 cup water
⅔ cups safflower or vegetable oil

ACCOMPANIMENTS
1 apple, chopped finely
1 banana, sliced
1 red pepper, cored, seeds removed, and
    chopped finely
1 carrot, grated
1 tomato, chopped finely
2 tbsps golden raisins
2 tbsps desiccated coconut
Half a cucumber, sliced, in 2 tbsps natural
    yogurt

**Stir-Fried Beef with Onions (top),
Shredded Beef with Vegetables (center
left) and Sesame Beef with Dates
(bottom).**

Heat a browning dish for 5 minutes on HIGH. Combine meat and oil and add to the dish. Cook 2 minutes on HIGH in 2 or 3 batches. Re-heat browning dish 2 minutes after each batch. Add the crushed chili pepper. Mix the soy sauce and stock and gradually stir into the cornstarch. Pour over the steak and cook 2-3 minutes. Add the celery and red pepper and mix together with the meat and sauce. Cook a further 1 minute on HIGH until the sauce has thickened but the vegetables are still crisp.

Five-Spice Beef with Broccoli

PREPARATION TIME: 15 minutes

COOKING TIME: 15 minutes

SERVES: 4 people

8oz sirloin or butt steak
1 clove garlic, crushed
½ tsp finely grated ginger
½ tsp five-spice powder
½ cup broccoli flowerets
Bunch of chives, cut into 1" lengths
2 tbsps peanut oil
½ tsp salt
1 tbsp dark soy sauce
½ cup hot water
2 tsps cornstarch, slaked in 1 tbsp cold
    water

Prepare fruit and vegetables. Heat wok, add oil and heat until warm. Add onion and garlic, and fry until golden brown. Remove garlic, and discard. Add steak and stir-fry until well browned all over. Add sultanas and stir in well. Add curry leaves, stir in, and cook for 5 minutes. Add cumin and coriander and stir. Cook a further 5 minutes. Add curry powder or paste and cook for 10 minutes. Add grated carrot, red pepper, apples, tomatoes, lemon rind and banana and mix in well. Add water. Cover and cook for 30 minutes. Stir in desiccated coconut and cook for a further 30 minutes. Add sugar and cook for another 20 minutes. Add more water as necessary. Add coconut cream and cook a further 20 minutes. Serve hot with boiled rice and accompaniments.

Peking Sweet Lamb

PREPARATION TIME: 1 hour

MICROWAVE COOKING TIME:
8-9 minutes plus 2 minutes standing time

SERVES: 4 people

1lb lamb fillet or meat from the leg, thinly sliced
2 tbsps hoisin sauce
1 tbsp rice wine
1 tbsp sesame oil
2 tbsps sugar
2 tbsps light soy sauce
2 tbsps vinegar
1 tbsp rice wine
1 tbsp cornstarch
½ cup plus 1 tbsp brown stock
1 tsp grated fresh ginger root

GARNISH
4 green onions, diagonally sliced

Mix the lamb, hoisin sauce and 1 tbsp rice wine. Set aside for 1 hour. Combine the sesame oil and sugar in a casserole dish. Heat for 1 minute on HIGH and stir. Add the lamb to the casserole, cover and cook 2 minutes on HIGH. Lower the setting to MEDIUM. Mix the remaining ingredients together, except for the garnish, and pour over the lamb. Cook for 5-7 minutes more, or until lamb is tender. Leave to stand for 2 minutes before serving, garnished with the sliced green onions.

Right: Guy's Curry (page 111).

POULTRY RECIPES

Roast Crispy Duck

PREPARATION TIME: 15-20 minutes plus 6-8 hours to dry

COOKING TIME: 1 hour 30 minutes

SERVES: 4-6 people

4½lb duck, prepared for cooking
1 cup water
6 large green onions cut into 2 inch lengths
5 tbsps maple syrup
½ tsp red food coloring
2½ tbsps ketchup

Wash the duck and pat it dry on a clean cloth. Ease the fingers between the skin and flesh of the duck, starting at the neck end and working the length of the bird. Put a stick or large skewer through the neck and the cavity of the duck to wedge it securely. This will make the duck easier to handle. Hold the duck over the sink and pour boiling water all over it. Pat the duck dry. Melt half the maple syrup and dissolve in the water. Stand the duck on a rack over a deep tray. Slowly pour the dissolved syrup over the duck. Pour the syrup liquid over the duck 3 or 4 times. Leave the duck in a cool place for 6-8 hours, or overnight, until the skin is dry. Remove the stick. Stand the duck on a rack in a roasting pan. Preheat the oven to 400°F, and cook for 30 minutes. Turn over and cook the underside for a further 30 minutes. Melt the remaining maple syrup with the ketchup and add the food coloring. Spread over the duck and cook for a further 30 minutes. (The duck should have a crisp, red skin.) Remove the duck skin in squares. Slice the duck flesh and serve with the skin on the top. Serve the following dip as an accompaniment.

DUCK DIP
4oz brown sugar
5 tbsps sweet bean paste
2½ tbsps sesame oil
½ cup water

Heat the wok and add the mixed ingredients. Cook for 3-4 minutes until the sugar has dissolved and the dip is smooth. Serve in individual cups.

Sliced Duck with Bamboo Shoots

PREPARATION TIME: 30 minutes

COOKING TIME: 10 minutes

SERVES: 2-3 people

2¼lb small duck
1 tsp monosodium glutamate (optional)
3 tsps cornstarch
2½ tbsps water
4oz broccoli, chopped
3 tbsps salad or olive oil
2-3 green onions, chopped
1 inch fresh root ginger, peeled and thinly sliced
1 clove garlic, peeled and finely chopped
⅔ cup bamboo shoots sliced
½ tsp fine granulated sugar
Salt and freshly ground black pepper to taste
5 tbsps chicken broth
2 tsps rice wine or sweet sherry
Few drops sesame oil

Cut the duck flesh into bite-size pieces, removing all the bones. Mix the MSG, with ⅔ of the cornstarch and 1 tbsp water. Stir into the duck. Marinate for 20 minutes. Cook the broccoli in boiling water for 1 minute. Drain thoroughly. Heat the wok and add the oil. Stir-fry the onions, ginger, garlic and bamboo shoots for 1-2 minutes. Add the duck pieces and stir-fry for 2-3 minutes. Add the sugar, salt and pepper to taste, broth rice wine and sesame oil. Stir-fry for 3 minutes. Add the remaining cornstarch and water blended together. Stir over the heat until the sauce thickens. Serve immediately, as a side dish.

Duck with Ginger and Pineapple

PREPARATION TIME: 20 minutes

COOKING TIME: 2 hours to 2 hours 45 minutes

SERVES: 4-6 people

½ inch fresh root ginger, peeled and crushed
1½ tbsps soy sauce
4½lb duck, prepared for cooking
Salt and freshly ground black pepper to taste
3 tbsps salad or olive oil
4 inches fresh root ginger, peeled and thinly sliced
¾ cup bean sprouts
3 green onions, chopped
2 carrots, peeled sliced and blanched in boiling water for 2 minutes
2 tsps brown sugar
1½ tbsps wine-flavored vinegar
1½ cups canned pineapple chunks in syrup
1¼ tbsps cornstarch mixed with 2½ tbsps water

Facing page: Sliced Duck with Bamboo Shoots (top), Duck with Ginger and Pineapple (bottom left) and Roast Crispy Duck (bottom right).

Mix together the crushed ginger, half of the soy sauce and salt and pepper to taste. Wash the duck and pat it dry. Rub the outside of the duck with salt and put on a wire rack in a roasting pan. Roast at 350°F, for 30 minutes. Brush the ginger and soy sauce mixture over the duck. Baste frequently with the sauces from the pan and roast for 2 hours, turning the bird occasionally to brown all sides. Remove and slice the duck in small pieces. Heat the oil in a wok and stir-fry the sliced ginger, bean sprouts, onions and carrots for 1-2 minutes. Add the duck slices and cook for 1 minute. Then add the brown sugar, vinegar and pineapple chunks in their syrup. Bring to the boil and cook for 2-3 minutes. Add the blended cornstarch and remaining soy sauce and cook until the sauce thickens. Serve as a main dish along with noodles or rice.

Empress Chicken

PREPARATION TIME: 30 minutes

MICROWAVE COOKING TIME:
15 minutes plus 3 minutes standing time

SERVES: 4 people

4 chicken wings
4 chicken breasts, skinned
12 dried Chinese mushrooms
½ cup soy sauce
2 cups chicken stock mixed with 3 tbsps cornstarch
1 tbsp sugar
2 pieces star anise
2 slices ginger root
1 tbsp rice wine
½ tsp salt
2 cans bamboo shoots, drained and cut in strips if thick
4 green onions, sliced

With a heavy cleaver, chop the chicken, through the bones, into large chunks. Remove any splinters of bone. Soak the mushrooms in hot water for 30 minutes. Drain and trim off the stems. Put the chicken, mushrooms and remaining ingredients, except the onions and bamboo shoots, into a deep casserole. Cover well and cook

15 minutes on HIGH or until the chicken is completely cooked. Add the bamboo shoots and sliced onions. Leave to stand 3 minutes and remove star anise before serving.

Chicken and Cashew Nuts

PREPARATION TIME: 15 minutes

COOKING TIME: 15 minutes

SERVES: 4 people

12oz chicken breast, sliced into 1 inch pieces
1 tbsp cornstarch

SEASONING
1 tsp salt
1 tsp sesame oil
1¼ tbsps light soy sauce
½ tsp brown sugar

Oil for deep frying and stir frying
¾ cup cashew nuts
2 green onions, chopped
1 small onion, peeled and cubed
1 inch fresh root ginger, peeled and sliced
2 cloves of garlic, sliced
1 cup pea pods
½ cup thinly sliced bamboo shoots

SAUCE
2 tsps cornstarch
1 tbsp Hoi Sin sauce
1 cup chicken broth
Pinch monosodium glutamate (optional)

Roll the chicken pieces in cornstarch. Discard the remaining cornstarch. Mix the seasoning ingredients together and pour over chicken. Leave to stand for 10 minutes. Heat oil for deep-frying in a wok and fry cashew nuts until golden brown. Remove the nuts and all but 2 tbsps of the oil; drain the nuts on kitchen paper. Heat the oil remaining in the wok and stir-fry the onions, ginger and garlic for 2-3 minutes. Add pea pods and bamboo shoots and stir-fry for 3 minutes. Remove the fried ingredients. Add 1 tbsp oil to the wok and fry the chicken for 3-4 minutes. Remove the chicken. Clean the wok and add a further 2 tbsps oil and return chicken, cashew nuts and fried onions etc. to the wok. Prepare the sauce by

mixing the cornstarch, Hoi Sin sauce, chicken broth and monosodium glutamate together. Pour over the chicken. Mix well and cook until the sauce thickens and becomes transparent. Serve hot with a chow mein dish. Alternatively, a few chunks of pineapple will add extra zest to the dish.

Golden Chicken with Walnuts

PREPARATION TIME: 20 minutes

MICROWAVE COOKING TIME:
7-9 minutes plus 2 minutes standing time

SERVES: 4 people

1lb chicken, skinned, boned and cut into bite-sized pieces
1 tbsp cornstarch
1 tbsp light soy sauce
1 tbsp sherry
1 cup stock
1 small can salted yellow beans
¾ cup walnuts, roughly chopped
½ small can sliced bamboo shoots

Combine chicken, cornstarch, soy sauce, sherry, stock, and yellow beans in a casserole dish. Cover and cook on HIGH for 7-9 minutes, stirring halfway through the cooking time. Once the sauce has thickened, add the walnuts and bamboo shoots. Leave to stand 2 minutes before serving.

Fried Shredded Chicken on Cabbage

PREPARATION TIME: 20 minutes

COOKING TIME: 12 minutes

SERVES: 4 people

1lb Chinese white cabbage, cut into 1 inch pieces
Pinch baking soda

Facing page: Empress Chicken (top) and Golden Chicken with Walnuts (bottom).

SEASONING

1¼ tbsps light soy sauce
1 tbsp cornstarch
¼ tsp sesame oil
¼ tsp freshly ground black pepper
½ tsp fine granulated sugar
½ tsp salt
1¼ tbsps water
1 tbsp salad or olive oil
Pinch monosodium glutamate (optional)

2 tbsps salad or olive oil
1 onion, peeled and roughly chopped
1 inch fresh root ginger, peeled and thinly
  sliced
1lb boned chicken breasts, shredded
4-6 mushrooms, sliced

SAUCE

3 tbsps chicken broth
¼ tsp sesame oil
1 tsp light soy sauce
1 tsp cornstarch
1 tsp monosodium glutamate (optional)

Wash cabbage and blanch in boiling
water with a pinch of baking soda for
2 minutes. Drain well and keep warm.

Mix the seasoning ingredients together.
Heat the wok and add the oil. Fry the
onions, ginger and chicken for 2-3
minutes. Add the mushrooms and fry
for further 2 minutes. Add the broth
and cook for 4-5 minutes. Mix the
sauce ingredients together and pour
over the chicken. Cook for 2 minutes.
Meanwhile place the cabbage on a
warmed dish as a bed for the sauced
chicken. Serve immediately.

Roast Spiced Duck

PREPARATION TIME: 3-4 hours to
dry, and 1 hour to glaze

COOKING TIME: 1 hour

SERVES: 4-6 people

4½lb duck, prepared for cooking
1 tsp five spice powder
1½ tsps salt
5 tbsps maple syrup
1½ tbsps wine-flavored vinegar
Salad or olive oil

Wash and dry the duck. Rub in the five spice powder and salt. Close the cavities of the duck by securing both ends with small skewers. Mix the maple syrup and vinegar together with a little water and bring to the boil. Spoon this liquid over the duck several times, collecting the liquid in a tray. Hang the duck by its neck for 3-4 hours to dry. Preheat the oven to 450°F. Place the duck in a roasting pan. Rub oil into the skin. Roast in the oven for 1 hour,

basting with any remaining maple syrup and vinegar liquid. If the duck is not quite tender, cook for a little longer. Slice the duck onto a warmed serving dish and serve immediately.

Inset far left: Stewed Chicken and Pineapple (page 122) (top right), Fried Shredded Chicken on Cabbage (page 116) (center left) and Chicken and Cashew Nuts (page 116) (bottom right). Roast Spiced Duck (top left), Roast Peking Duck (page 120) (left) and Steamed Duck in Wine Sauce (bottom).

Steamed Duck in Wine Sauce

PREPARATION TIME: 20 minutes

COOKING TIME: 30 hours 30 minutes

SERVES: 4-6 people

4½lb duck, prepared for cooking
Generous ½ cup Kao Liang wine, or mild red wine
½ tsp monosodium glutamate (optional)
1 inch fresh root ginger, peeled and thinly sliced
3 green onions, chopped
1 tsp salt
1 tsp fine granulated sugar
1¼ tsps cornstarch

Place the duck in a large pot. Add water to cover and boil for 5-7 minutes. Remove the duck and drain well. Mix all the remaining ingredients together apart from the cornstarch. Place the duck in a deep dish and stand over a steamer. Pour the wine mixture over the duck. Cover and steam for 2-3 hours until the duck is quite tender. Remove the duck and strain the cooking liquid. Place the duck on a serving dish, either whole or cut into slices. Blend the cooking liquid with the cornstarch. Bring to the boil and stir until thickened. Pour over the duck. Serve immediately.

Diced Chicken and Peppers

PREPARATION TIME: 20 minutes

MICROWAVE COOKING TIME:
8½-10½ minutes plus 2 minutes
standing time

SERVES: 4 people

2 tbsps oil
1 clove garlic, minced
1lb chicken, skinned, boned and diced
2 green peppers, diced
1 small red chili pepper, diced
½ small can bamboo shoots, diced
1 tsp cornstarch
2 tbsps white wine
2 tbsp soy sauce
4 tbsps chicken stock
Pinch sugar (optional)
Salt

Heat oil 30 seconds on HIGH in a
large casserole dish. Add the garlic
and cook 30 seconds on HIGH. Add
the chicken and stir to coat with oil.
Add the chili pepper, cornstarch,
wine, soy sauce and stock. Stir well
and cover the dish. Cook 7-9
minutes on HIGH, stirring halfway
through the cooking time. Add the
green pepper, sugar (if using) and salt
if needed. Cook 30 seconds on
HIGH, add bamboo shoots and leave
to stand, covered, 2 minutes before
serving. Serve with fried or plain
boiled rice.

Roast Peking Duck

PREPARATION TIME: 15 minutes plus
2-3 hours to dry out the skin

COOKING TIME: 1 hour 20 minutes

SERVES: 4-6 people

4½lb duck, prepared for cooking
4½ cups boiling water
2½ tbsps maple syrup
1 cup water
2-3 seedless oranges, peeled and cut into
 rings
2 tbsps salad or olive oil
Salt and freshly ground black pepper

SAUCE
2½ tsps cornstarch

5 tbsps water or broth
Pinch monosodium glutamate (optional)
2½ tsps light soy sauce
1 tsp rice wine or dry sherry

TO GARNISH
4 green onions, cut into 2 inch lengths

Wash and dry the duck. Put a stick or
skewer through the neck and the cavity
of the duck so that it is easier to
handle. Hold the bird over the sink and
pour the boiling water over it. Hang
the duck up to dry. Melt the syrup and
water together and spoon over the
duck several times, catching the liquid
on a drip tray each time. Leave the
duck to dry for 2-3 hours in a cool
place. Save any liquid that drops off.
Preheat the oven to 400°F. Place the
duck, breast side down, in a roasting
pan and roast for 30 minutes. Lift out
the duck. Put the orange rings into the
pan and sit the duck on top, breast side
uppermost. Baste with the oil and
season with salt and pepper. Roast for a
further 45-50 minutes until tender.
Cut off the duck joints and slice the
breast meat. Arrange with the orange
slices on a serving dish and keep warm.

TO MAKE THE SAUCE
Mix the sauce ingredients together and
add any reserved maltose liquid. Bring
to the boil gently, stirring, until the
sauce thickens. Pour over the cooked
duck and sprinkle with the onions.

Peking Duck with Pancakes

PREPARATION TIME: for duck 2-3 hours; for pancakes 6 minutes

COOKING TIME: for duck 1 hour 20 minutes; for pancakes 15 minutes

SERVES: 6-8 people

4½lb Peking duck, roasted (see recipe)
16-20 green onions, sliced into 3 inch pieces

PANCAKES (PO PING)
1lb all-purpose flour
Pinch salt
1¼ tbsps salad or olive oil
1 tsp sesame oil
Tepid water for kneading
Flour for rolling

TO MAKE PANCAKES
Sift the flour and salt into a mixing bowl. Make a well in the center and add the oils and water, a little at a time,

Facing page: Diced Chicken and Peppers. This page: Peking Duck with Pancakes.

and work in the flour. Make a pliable dough. Remove from the bowl and knead well for 2-3 minutes. Cover with a damp, clean cloth and allow to rest for 10 minutes. Knead again for 1 minute and divide the dough into 16-20 even-sized balls. Roll each ball in flour and roll out into a 4-6 inch circle. Place a skillet on the heat and when moderately hot place the rolled circle of dough on it; cook for ½-1 minute. Little bubbles will appear; flip over and allow to cook for 1-1½ minutes. Pick the pancake up and check whether little brown specs have appeared on the undersides; if not, then cook for few seconds more. Use a clean tea towel to press the pancakes gently, this will circulate the steam and cook the

pancakes. Prepare the rest of the pancakes in the same way and keep them stacked, wrapped in foil to keep them warm.

TO MAKE DIP
5 tbsps brown sugar
4 tbsps bean paste (sweet)
1 tbsp sesame oil
1 tbsp olive oil or peanut oil
1 cup water

OTHER DIPS, READY PREPARED
4 tbsps Hoi Sin sauce
4 tbsps Chinese barbecue sauce

Mix sugar, bean paste and water together. Warm the wok, add the oil and then the sugar mixture. Bring to boil and, when the sugar has melted, remove and put in a bowl. Place the duck on a cutting board and cut thin slices from the breast area and thighs. Place a pancake on an individual plate, cover with a slice of duck and a few strips of onion, spread on a dip of your choice, roll up like a pancake and eat. To make very crisp duck, cut duck into large joints and deep-fry them till crispy.

Chicken Chow Mein

| PREPARATION TIME: 30 minutes |
| COOKING TIME: 20 minutes |
| SERVES: 4 people |

1lb egg noodles or spaghetti, broken into
    small pieces
1 onion, peeled and thinly sliced
½ cup mushrooms, sliced
3 green onions, chopped
2 cloves of garlic, peeled and chopped
Salt to taste
Pinch monosodium glutamate
4 tbsps salad or olive oil
1½ cups chicken meat, finely shredded
2½ tbsps light soy sauce
1 tsp fine granulated sugar
1 tbsp rice wine or dry sherry
⅓ cup chicken broth

Cook the noodles in boiling, salted water for 4-5 minutes until tender. Drain and rinse under cold water. Drain once again and add 2 tbsps oil; mix well to prevent the noodles from sticking together. Heat 2 tbsps oil in a wok and fry the onions and garlic for 2 minutes. Add chicken and stir-fry for 3-4 minutes. Add mushrooms. Sprinkle over the wine, sugar, soy sauce, monosodium glutamate and salt to taste. Cook until the mixture is fairly dry. Add noodles and stir well to mix. Sprinkle over the broth and cook once again until dry. Serve with chili sauce and dark soy sauce. ½ cup sliced green beans, ⅓ cup lightly cooked peas or ⅓ cup shredded carrot may also be added, along with the chicken pieces.

Stewed Chicken and Pineapple

| PREPARATION TIME: 30 minutes |
| COOKING TIME: 15 minutes |
| SERVES: 4 people |

SEASONING
2½ tbsps light soy sauce
1 tbsp salad or olive oil

1 tbsp cornstarch
1 tsp salt
½ tsp sesame oil
2 tbsps water

1½lbs boned chicken breast, cut into cubes

SAUCE
1½ tsps cornstarch
1 cup water or chicken broth
2½ tsps dark soy sauce
Salt to taste

2 tbsps salad or olive oil
1 onion, peeled and cut into chunks
2 green onions, finely chopped
1 inch fresh root ginger, peeled and thinly
    sliced
4-5 pineapple rings, cut into chunks

Mix the seasoning ingredients together. Add the cubed chicken and marinate for 10-12 minutes. Mix the sauce ingredients together in a bowl. Heat the oil in a wok and fry the onions for 2 minutes until just tender. Add the drained chicken and fry for 3-4 minutes. Add the root ginger and fry for 1 minute. Add any remaining marinade and the sauce ingredients and bring to the boil. Cook, stirring, until the sauce thickens then add the pineapple chunks. Heat through. Remove from the heat and serve with fried rice.

Tangerine Peel Chicken

| PREPARATION TIME: 30 minutes |
| COOKING TIME: 12-15 minutes |
| SERVES: 4 people |

1lb boned chicken breast, cut into 1 inch
    pieces

SEASONING
½ tsp salt
1½ tsps brown sugar
½ tsp monosodium glutamate (optional)
1 tsp dark soy sauce
2½ tsps light soy sauce
1 tsp rice wine or dry sherry
2½ tsps brown vinegar
1 tsp sesame oil
2 tsps cornstarch

Oil for deep frying
1-2 red or green chilies, chopped

½ inch fresh root ginger, peeled and finely
    chopped
2 inches dried tangerine peel, coarsely
    ground or crumbled
2 green onions, finely chopped

SAUCE
½ tsp cornstarch
1-2 tbsps water or broth

Mix the chicken pieces with the seasoning ingredients and stir well. Leave to marinate for 10-15 minutes. Remove the chicken pieces and reserve the marinade. Heat wok and add the oil for deep frying. Once it starts to smoke add the chicken pieces and fry for 4-5 minutes until golden. Drain chicken on kitchen paper. Tip off the oil, leaving 1 tbsp oil in the wok, and stir-fry the chilies, ginger, tangerine peel and onions for 2-3 minutes. When they begin to color add the chicken and stir-fry for 1 minute. Mix the reserved marinade with the sauce ingredients and pour over the chicken. Stir and cook for 2-3 minutes until the sauce thickens and the chicken is tender. Serve imediately.

Sweet and Sour Chicken

| PREPARATION TIME: 30 minutes |
| COOKING TIME: 20 minutes |
| SERVES: 3-4 people |

½ tsp salt
3 tsp cornstarch
2 chicken breasts, cut into ½ inch cubes
1 onion, peeled and roughly chopped into
    ½ inch pieces
¼ cup sliced bamboo shoots
1 green pepper, seeded and thinly sliced
1 inch fresh root ginger, peeled and thinly
    sliced
2 carrots, scraped and thinly sliced into 1
    inch long pieces
1 garlic clove, peeled and chopped
2 tbsps salad or olive oil

Facing page: Tangerine Peel Chicken (top), Sweet and Sour Chicken (center left) and Chicken Chow Mein (bottom).

BATTER
1 cup all-purpose flour
1 tbsp cornstarch
1 small egg

Oil for deep frying

SAUCE
1 tbsp brown sugar
1¼ tbsps wine-flavored vinegar
1¼ tbsps soy sauce
1 tbsp ketchup
2 cups chicken broth
Pinch monosodium glutamate (optional)
2½ tsps cornstarch

Mix salt and cornstarch and roll chicken pieces in it. Make the batter by mixing the sieved flour and cornstarch with the egg and sufficient water to make a thick batter. Beat well. Heat oil for deep-frying. Dip the chicken pieces into the batter and deep-fry until golden brown and crisp. Drain on absorbent paper and keep warm. Heat the 2 tbsps oil in a wok and stir-fry the onion, ginger and garlic for 2-3 minutes. Add the carrots and fry for 2 minutes. Add the green pepper and fry for 2 minutes. Add bamboo shoots, season with salt and stir well. Mix all the sauce ingredients together. Pour over the cooked vegetables. Cook 2-3 minutes until the sauce thickens. The sauce should become transparent. Arrange fried chicken pieces on a serving dish and pour the sweet and sour sauce over them. Serve as a side dish.

Chicken Fry with Sauce

PREPARATION TIME: 20 minutes

COOKING TIME: about 24 minutes

SERVES: 4 people

1 tbsp cooked oil
1 tsp sesame oil
2 tbsps sesame seeds

SAUCE
2 cloves garlic, minced
2 green onions, finely chopped or minced
1 tsp Chinese black vinegar, or brown vinegar
3½ tbsps dark soy sauce
1 tsp light soy sauce
½ tsp monosodium glutamate (optional)
½ tsp salt
1½ tsps fine granulated sugar

8 chicken thighs, or 1lb chicken, cut into small joints

Heat the wok and add the oils. Stir-fry the sesame seeds till they change color to golden brown. Remove to a dish. Mix sauce ingredients together and add the sesame seeds. Wipe the wok and add the chicken. Add sufficient water to cover, and cook for 20 minutes until the chicken is tender. De-bone the

chicken and quickly cut into bite-size pieces. Arrange the chicken on a plate and spoon the sauce over the top. Serve immediately.

Chicken and Mushrooms

PREPARATION TIME: 15 minutes, plus 10 minutes to marinate

COOKING TIME: 10-12 minutes

SERVES: 3-4 people

SEASONING
½ tsp salt
2½ tbsps light soy sauce

2 tsps cornstarch
1 tsp rice wine or dry sherry
Pinch monosodium glutamate (optional)

½lb chicken breast, cut into bite-size pieces

SAUCE
Salt to taste
Freshly ground black pepper to taste
1¼ tbsps light soy sauce

Chicken Fry with Sauce (below left), Chicken Green Chili (page 133) (below center) and Chicken and Mushrooms (below right).

1 cup chicken broth
2 tsps cornstarch
1 tsp oyster sauce

2 tbsps salad or olive oil
1 onion, peeled and chopped
1 clove of garlic, sliced
½ inch fresh root ginger, peeled and thinly sliced
3 dried black mushrooms, soaked and sliced
½ cup open mushrooms, sliced
½ cup button mushrooms, sliced

Mix the seasoning ingredients together. Marinate the chicken in the seasoning

2 tbsps redcurrant jelly
1 tsp arrowroot
1 tbsp cold water
Salt
Pepper

GARNISH
Watercress
Slivers of orange peel

Pare the rind of 2 oranges and cut
into fine shreds. Blanch in hot water
and set aside for garnish. Extract
juice from 2 oranges. Cut peel and
pith from 1 orange, and then slice
into rounds, or cut flesh into sections
if preferred. Wash duck and dry well
with paper towels. Heat wok, and
add oil and butter. When hot, add
duck, and brown all over. Remove
from wok and, using poultry shears
or a chopper, cut duck in half
lengthwise and then cut each half
into 1″ strips. Return duck to wok,
and add stock, red wine, redcurrant
jelly, orange juice and rind, and salt
and pepper to taste. Bring to boil,
reduce heat, cover and simmer gently
for 20 minutes. Add orange slices,
and simmer a further 10 minutes, or
until duck is cooked. If sauce needs
to be thickened, mix arrowroot with
cold water and add to sauce. Bring to
the boil, and simmer for 3 minutes.
Garnish with slivers of orange peel
and watercress.

Lacquered Duck with Plum Sauce

PREPARATION TIME: 25 minutes

MICROWAVE COOKING TIME:
43-48 minutes plus 10 minutes
standing time

SERVES: 4 people

SAUCE
See Plum Sauce recipe

GLAZE
¼ cup honey
4 tbsps soy sauce
5lb duckling

**This page: Duck with Orange. Facing
page: Lacquered Duck with Plum
Sauce.**

mixture for 10 minutes. Mix the sauce
ingredients together. Heat the oil in a
wok and fry the onion, garlic and ginger
for 2-3 minutes. Remove and keep on
one side. Fry the drained chicken in the
remaining oil for 4 minutes. Add the
mushrooms and stir-fry for 1 minute.
Add a little extra oil if necessary.
Return the fried onion mixture to the
wok and stir-fry until well mixed. Pour
the blended sauce ingredients into the
wok and cook gently until the sauce
thickens. Serve piping hot.

Duck with Orange

PREPARATION TIME: 30 minutes

COOKING TIME: 50 minutes

SERVES: 4 people

1 small duck
1 tbsp butter or margarine
1 tbsp oil
3 oranges
1¼ cups light chicken stock
⅓ cup red wine

2 tbsps oil
1lb chicken breasts, skinned, boned and
    cut into thin slivers
2 tsps cornstarch
3 tbsps rice wine
3 tbsps light soy sauce
2 tbsps oyster sauce
4 tbsps chicken stock
4oz pea pods
Dash sesame oil
Salt and pepper

Heat the oil 30 seconds on HIGH in
a large casserole dish. Mix the
remaining ingredients except the pea
pods and pour over the chicken.
Cover and cook 7-9 minutes on
HIGH, stirring halfway through the
cooking time. Add the pea pods,
re-cover the dish and cook 30
seconds on HIGH. Leave to stand
for 2 minutes before serving. Serve
with rice.

Chicken with Hoisin Sauce and Cashews

1lb chicken, skinned, boned and cut into
    bite-sized pieces
1 tbsp cornstarch
1 cup stock
1 tbsp light soy sauce
1 clove garlic, finely minced
1 tbsp white wine
4 tbsps hoisin sauce
½ cup roasted cashew nuts
4 green onions, diagonally sliced

Combine the chicken with all the
ingredients except the nuts and

GARNISH
¼ cup toasted, chopped almonds
Green onion brushes (see Introduction)

Brush the duckling with the honey
and soy sauce glaze. Cook on rack on
HIGH for 10 minutes. Turn over,
brush with the glaze and cook 10
minutes on HIGH. Turn again and
brush with some of the plum sauce.
Lower the setting to MEDIUM and
cook 15-30 minutes or until tender.
Cover and leave to stand 10 minutes

before cutting into 8 pieces with a
cleaver or poultry shears. Pour over
remaining plum sauce and sprinkle
over the almonds. Garnish with
onion brushes and serve with rice.

Chicken with Pea Pods

This page: **Sesame Chicken with Garlic Sauce (page 130) (top) and Lemon Chicken (page 138) (bottom). Facing page: Chicken with Pea Pods (top) and Chicken with Hoisin Sauce and Cashews (bottom).**

onions. Put into a casserole dish, cover and cook on HIGH for 7-9 minutes, stirring halfway through the cooking time. Once the sauce has thickened and the cornstarch has cleared, add the nuts and the green onions. Re-cover the dish and leave to stand 2 minutes before serving. Serve with rice.

Steamed Chicken

PREPARATION TIME: 20-30 minutes	
COOKING TIME: 15-20 minutes	
SERVES: 4 people	

1½lb boned chicken

SEASONING
1¼ tbsps light soy sauce
1 tsp brown sugar
1 tsp salt
1 tbsp cornstarch
2 tbsps oil or cooked oil
½ tsp monosodium glutamate (optional)

4oz dried mushrooms, soaked in boiling water for 5 minutes and sliced, (or ordinary mushrooms)
½ inch fresh root ginger, peeled and sliced
4 green onions, finely chopped
2 tbsps broth or water, if needed

Cut the chicken into 1 inch pieces. Mix the seasoning ingredients together and mix with the chicken. Leave to marinate for 15 minutes. Place a plate in a steamer and put the chicken, mushrooms, ginger, half the onion and the broth on top. Steam over boiling water for 15-20 minutes. Serve with the remaining onions sprinkled over the chicken. The steaming can also be done on a greased lotus leaf or a banana leaf. The flavor is quite stunning.

Sesame Chicken with Garlic Sauce

PREPARATION TIME: 30 minutes	
MICROWAVE COOKING TIME: 7-9 minutes plus 2 minutes standing time	
SERVES: 4 people	

6 chicken thighs, skinned
1 tbsp sesame oil
4 cloves garlic, finely minced
1 tsp finely chopped ginger root
1½ tsp brown sugar
2 tbsps dark soy sauce
½ cup chicken stock
½ tsp black pepper
2 tsps cornstarch
6 green onions, sliced
4 tbsps sesame seeds
Salt

Bone the chicken thighs and cut the meat into thin strips or small pieces. Combine the garlic, sesame oil, ginger root, sugar, soy sauce and pepper and pour over the chicken in a shallow dish. Cover and refrigerate for 30 minutes. Mix the cornstarch and stock, add to the chicken and marinade and stir well. Cover the dish and cook on HIGH for 4-9 minutes, stirring halfway through the cooking time. Add the sesame seeds and onions and leave to stand, covered, 2 minutes before serving. Serve with rice or Chinese noodles.

Chicken Chop Suey

PREPARATION TIME: 30 minutes	
COOKING TIME: 15 minutes	
SERVES: 4 people	

2½ tbsps light soy sauce
1 tsp brown sugar
Salt to taste
1lb boned chicken, cut into 1 inch pieces
2 tbsps salad or olive oil
1 onion, cut into chunks
2½ cups bean sprouts
2 tsps sesame oil
¼ tsp monosodium glutamate (optional)
1 tbsp cornstarch
1 cup chicken broth

Mix the soy sauce with the sugar and salt and add the chicken pieces. Allow to marinate for 5 minutes. Drain the chicken and reserve the marinade. Heat the wok and add the oil. Fry the chicken for 2-3 minutes. Remove the chicken. Fry the onions for 2-3 minutes and add the bean sprouts. Stir-fry for 4-5 minutes. Return the chicken to the pan and add the sesame oil. Dissolve

the monosodium glutamate and the cornstarch in the broth and pour over the chicken mixture along with the reserved marinade. Cook for 2-3 minutes, stirring, until the sauce thickens.

Deep-Fried Crispy Chicken

PREPARATION TIME: 3 hours	
COOKING TIME: 13-14 minutes	
SERVES: 4 people	

3-3½lb chicken, prepared for cooking

SEASONING
1 tsp salt
½ tsp five spice powder
2 tbsps maple syrup
2 tbsps brown vinegar
⅔ cup wine-flavored vinegar

Oil for deep frying

Wash the chicken and hang it up by a hook to drain and dry. The skin will dry quickly. Pour boiling water over the chicken 4-5 times to partially cook the skin. This will make the skin crisp during frying. Rub salt and five spice powder well inside the chicken cavity. Dissolve the maple syrup and vinegars in a pan over a gentle heat. Pour over the chicken. Repeat several times, catching the syrup solution in a drip tray. Leave the chicken to hang and dry for 1½-2 hours, until the skin is smooth and shiny. Heat the oil for deep frying. Deep-fry the chicken for 10 minutes. Ladle hot oil carefully over the chicken continually, until the chicken is deep brown in color. (The skin puffs out slightly.) Cook for a further 3-4 minutes and remove from the oil. Drain on absorbent paper. Cut into small pieces and serve with a dip.

Facing page: Chicken Chop Suey (top left), Steamed Chicken (center right) and Deep-Fried Crispy Chicken (bottom left).

Stir-Fried Chicken with Yellow Bean Paste

PREPARATION TIME:
1 hour 10 minutes

COOKING TIME: 20 minutes

SERVES: 4 people

1lb chicken breasts, sliced thinly
2 tbsps oil
2 tbsps yellow bean paste
1 tsp sugar
1 egg white, lightly beaten
1 tbsp rice vinegar
1 tbsp light soy sauce
1 tbsp cornstarch
Salt
Pepper

GARNISH
Green onion flowers (cut green onions
  into 2" lengths. Carefully cut into fine
  shreds, keeping one end intact, and then
  soak in cold water until curling).

Mix together lightly beaten egg-
white, cornstarch, and salt and
pepper. Place chicken in a bowl and
pour over mixture. Toss together to
coat well. Set aside in a cool place for
at least 1 hour. Combine vinegar, soy
sauce and sugar. Remove chicken,
and set egg mixture aside. Heat wok,
and add oil. When hot, stir-fry
chicken until lightly browned.
Remove from wok. Add bean paste
to wok and stir-fry for 1 minute. Add
vinegar mixture and stir in well.
Return chicken to pan, and fry gently
for 2 minutes. Finally, add egg
mixture, and simmer until sauce
thickens, stirring all the time. Garnish
with green onion flowers. Serve
immediately with boiled rice.

Chicken with Mango
(above) and Stir-Fried
Chicken with Yellow
Bean Paste (bottom
right).

Chicken with Mango

PREPARATION TIME: 5 minutes

COOKING TIME: 30 minutes

SERVES: 4 people

4 chicken breasts, cut into shreds
2 ripe mangoes, sliced, or 1 can sliced
  mangoes, drained
4 green onions, sliced diagonally
½ tsp ground cinnamon
1 tsp grated ginger
1 tbsp light soy sauce
1 chicken bouillon cube
⅔ cup water
2 tbsps oil
2 tbsps sweet sherry
1 tsp sugar
Salt
Pepper

Heat wok and add oil. Add ginger and cinnamon, and fry for 30 seconds. Add chicken and green onions, and stir-fry for 5 minutes. Add light soy sauce, crumbled chicken bouillon cube, water and sugar, and bring to boil. Add salt and pepper to taste, and simmer for 15 minutes. Add mangoes and sherry, and simmer, uncovered, until sauce has reduced and thickened. Serve hot with boiled rice.

Chicken Green Chili

PREPARATION TIME: 10 minutes, plus 10 minutes to marinate

COOKING TIME: 10 minutes

SERVES: 4 people

SAUCE
1 tsp light soy sauce
1 tsp dark soy sauce
Salt to taste
2 tsps cornstarch
1 tsp sesame oil
1 tsp vinegar
1 cup chicken broth

SEASONING
Salt to taste
Freshly ground black pepper to taste
Pinch monosodium glutamate (optional)
2½ tbsps dark soy sauce
1¼ tbsps light soy sauce
1 tsp cornstarch
2 tsp rice wine or dry sherry

1lb boned chicken, cut into bite-size pieces
3 tbsps salad or olive oil
3 green onions, chopped
1 inch fresh root ginger, peeled and sliced
2 cloves of garlic, peeled and sliced
1 green pepper, seeded and chopped
2-3 green chilies, sliced lengthwise

This page: Duck with Pineapple (page 140). Facing page: Singapore Chicken.

Mix the sauce ingredients together. Mix the seasoning ingredients together and add the chicken. Marinate for 10 minutes. Drain the chicken and discard the liquid. Heat 1 tbsp oil and stir-fry the onions, ginger and garlic for 2 minutes. Remove to a dish. Add the remaining oil and stir-fry the chicken for 3 minutes. Add the blended green peppers and chilies and stir-fry for

2 minutes. Add the onion mixture and the well-blended sauce ingredients and cook for 3-4 minutes until the sauce thickens. Serve immediately.

Singapore Chicken

PREPARATION TIME: 20 minutes

MICROWAVE COOKING TIME: 11 minutes plus 2 minutes standing time

SERVES: 4 people

2 tbsps oil
2 tsps curry powder

Chili Sichuan Chicken (top) and Honey
Soy Chicken Wings (page 138) (bottom).
Facing page: Duck with Five Spices
(page 140) (top) and Duck with Onions
(pae 138) (bottom).

1 tbsp cornstarch
1 cup bean sprouts
Dash soy sauce
Salt and pepper

Heat the oil in a large casserole dish
for 30 seconds on HIGH. Add the
curry powder, and cook 30 seconds
on HIGH. Add the chicken, cover
the dish and cook 5 minutes on
HIGH. Add the onion, mix the
cornstarch with the reserved
pineapple and orange juice and add
to the chicken. Cover and cook
5 minutes on HIGH, stirring
occasionally after 1 minute. When
the sauce thickens, add the
pineapple, orange segments and bean
sprouts. Leave to stand 2 minutes
before serving. Serve with fried or
plain boiled rice.

Chili Sichuan Chicken

PREPARATION TIME: 40 minutes

COOKING TIME: 20 minutes

SERVES: 4 people

4 chicken breasts, sliced thinly
1 clove garlic, crushed
1 green pepper, cored, seeds removed, and
    diced
1 red pepper, cored, seeds removed, and
    diced
1 red chili pepper, seeds removed, and
    sliced finely
1 green chili pepper, seeds removed, and
    sliced finely
1 tsp chili sauce
1 tbsp light soy sauce
1 tsp Chinese wine, or dry sherry
½ tsp cornstarch
Salt
Pepper
⅔ cup peanut oil, for deep frying

SAUCE
1¼ cups chicken stock
2 tsps cornstarch
1 tsp Chinese wine, or dry sherry

1lb chicken, skinned, boned and cut into
    bite-sized pieces
1 large onion, cut in large pieces
1 8oz can pineapple pieces, juice reserved
1 10oz can mandarin orange segments,
    juice reserved

Mix together 1 tsp wine, ½ tsp
cornstarch, light soy sauce, and a
pinch of salt and pepper. Pour over
chicken and mix well. Leave to
marinate for at least 30 minutes.
Heat oil for deep frying in wok.

When hot, toss in sliced chicken and fry until just coloring and cooked through. Drain well. Carefully remove all but 1 tbsp of oil from wok. Heat, and when hot, add garlic, green and red peppers, green and red chili peppers, and chili sauce. Fry gently for 2 minutes. Stir 2 tbsps of chicken stock into cornstarch, then pour remaining chicken stock and wine into wok. Add cornstarch mixture and stir well, until sauce boils and thickens. Add chicken, and toss until heated through. Serve with rice.

Lemon Chicken

PREPARATION TIME: 30 minutes

MICROWAVE COOKING TIME: 7-9 minutes plus 2 minutes standing time

SERVES: 4 people

4 chicken breasts, skinned, boned and cut into thin strips
4 tbsps soy sauce
2 tsps dry sherry or shao-hsing wine
Salt and pepper

SAUCE
3 tbsps salted black beans
2 tbsps water
6 tbsps lemon juice
1 cup chicken stock
4 tbsps sugar
1 tsp sesame oil
3 tbsps cornstarch
2 cloves garlic, finely minced
¼ tsp red pepper flakes

GARNISH
Lemon slices

Mix chicken with marinade ingredients, cover and refrigerate 30 minutes. Crush the black beans, combine with the water and leave to stand until ready to use. Combine remaining sauce ingredients in a shallow dish. Add the chicken, marinade and black beans, cover and cook on HIGH for 7-9 minutes, stirring halfway through the cooking time. Once the cornstarch has cleared, leave the chicken to stand, covered for 2 minutes before serving. Garnish with lemon slices and serve with rice.

Honey Soy Chicken Wings

PREPARATION TIME: 5 minutes

COOKING TIME: 30 minutes

SERVES: 4 people

1lb chicken wings
½ tsp salt
2 tbsps peanut oil
¼ cup light soy sauce
2 tbsps clear honey
1 clove garlic, crushed
1 tsp ginger, freshly grated
1 tsp sesame seeds

Heat wok, add oil, and when hot, add chicken wings and fry for 10 minutes. Pour off excess oil carefully. Add soy sauce, honey, sesame seeds, garlic, grated ginger and salt. Reduce heat, and gently simmer for 20 minutes, turning occasionally. Serve hot or cold with rice.

Duck with Onions

PREPARATION TIME: 20 minutes

MICROWAVE COOKING TIME: 42-58 minutes plus 10 minutes standing time

SERVES: 4 people

5lb duck
⅓ cup soy sauce
2 pieces fresh ginger root, peeled and grated
3 tbsps white wine
1 tbsp sugar
2 tbsps cornstarch dissolved in 2 tbsps water
10 green onions
1 small can sliced bamboo shoots
4 Chinese mushrooms, soaked and sliced
Salt

Combine the soy sauce and grated ginger and brush over the breast side of the duck. Place the duck on a rack and cook for 10 minutes on HIGH. Turn over, brush with the soy sauce and cook 10 minutes on HIGH. Place in a very large casserole or bowl. Add 3 green onions, wine and 1 cup water. Cover the bowl or casserole and cook 15-30 minutes or until tender.

Remove the duck and keep warm. Discard the cooked onions. Skim off fat from the cooking liquid and mix a spoonful of the liquid with the cornstarch and water and the sugar. Add the bamboo shoots, mushrooms and remaining onions, sliced, to the sauce. Cook for 2-3 minutes on HIGH until thick and clear. Cut the duck into 8 pieces and pour over the sauce to serve.

Chicken Livers with Peppers

PREPARATION TIME: 30 minutes

COOKING TIME: 15 minutes

SERVES: 4 people

1lb chicken livers
4 Chinese mushrooms
1 green pepper
1 red pepper
1 tbsp rice vinegar
2 tsps sugar
1oz fresh ginger
1 small leek
3 tbsps vegetable oil
1 onion

GARNISH
2 green onion flowers (trim and slice lengthwise, keep one end intact, and leave in cold water in refrigerator until curling)

Soak mushrooms in hot water for 20 minutes. Clean and trim chicken livers, and blanch in boiling water for 3 minutes. Drain and slice. Peel and finely slice ginger. Mix vinegar and sugar, and add ginger, and set aside. Clean and trim leek and cut into thin rings. Peel and slice onion and cut into strips. Core and remove seeds from peppers, and cut into strips. Drain mushrooms, remove hard stalks, and cut caps into thin slices. Heat wok, add oil, and, when hot, add mushrooms, onion, leek and peppers, and stir-fry for 5 minutes. Remove and set aside. Add liver and

Facing page: Chicken Livers with Peppers.

ginger mixture. Stir-fry for a further 5 minutes, return vegetable mixture to wok and heat through. Serve garnished with green onion flowers.

Sesame Fried Chicken

PREPARATION TIME: 10 minutes

COOKING TIME: 30 minutes

SERVES: 4 people

1lb chicken breasts, or 4 good-sized pieces
¾ cup flour
1 tsp salt
1 tsp pepper
¼ cup sesame seeds
2 tsps paprika
1 egg, beaten, with 1 tbsp water
3 tbsps olive oil

Sift flour onto a sheet of wax paper and stir in salt, pepper, paprika and sesame seeds. Dip chicken breasts in egg and water mixture, then coat well in seasoned flour. Heat wok, add oil and, when hot, fry the chicken breasts until golden brown on both sides. Turn heat down, and cook gently for 10 minutes on each side. Serve hot with rice.

Duck with Five Spices

PREPARATION TIME: 20 minutes

MICROWAVE COOKING TIME: 30 minutes

SERVES: 4 people

5lb duckling
½ cup rice wine
½ cup light soy sauce
2 tbsps honey
1 clove garlic, finely minced
1 tbsp five-spice powder
4 tbsps chicken stock

2 tbsps cornstarch, dissolved in 3 tbsps water

Remove the meat from the legs and breast of the duck. Take off the skin and cut the meat into bite-sized pieces. Combine with the remaining ingredients, except the cornstarch and water, in a casserole. Cover the dish and cook on HIGH for 10 minutes. Reduce the setting and cook an additional 20 minutes on MEDIUM. Check the level of liquid from time to time and add more stock or water if necessary. When the duck is cooked, add a few spoonfuls of the cooking liquid to the cornstarch and water. Return the mixture to the casserole and cook on HIGH for 2-3 minutes to thicken the sauce. Serve with rice or stir-fried vegetables. Garnish with Chinese parsley if desired.

Duck with Pineapple

PREPARATION TIME: 20 minutes

MICROWAVE COOKING TIME: 9-10 minutes

SERVES: 4 people

SAUCE
See Pineapple Sauce recipe

5lb duckling
2 tbsps oil
2 tbsps soy sauce

GARNISH
4 chives, shredded

Skin the duck and remove the leg and breast meat. Cut into thin slivers. Heat a browning dish 5 minutes on HIGH. Toss the oil and duck together, and add to the browning dish. Cook, uncovered,

4 minutes on HIGH. Add the soy sauce, cover the dish and reduce the setting to MEDIUM. Cook a further 3 minutes or until duck is tender. Remove duck to a serving dish and keep warm. Coat with the pineapple sauce and sprinkle on the chives. Serve with rice.

Chicken Curry (Mild)

PREPARATION TIME: 10 minutes

COOKING TIME: 40 minutes

SERVES: 4 people

3lbs chicken
1 tbsp peanut oil
1 onion, peeled and finely chopped
2 cloves garlic, crushed
½ tsp grated ginger
2 tsps curry powder
½ tsp salt
1 tbsp vinegar
⅔ cup milk
⅔ cup coconut cream

Cut chicken into small pieces: breast-meat into 4 pieces, thigh-meat into 2 pieces, and wings separated at joints. Heat oil until hot. Reduce heat. Add onion, garlic and ginger and cook gently, stirring continuously. Cook for 10 minutes, or until onion is soft and a golden brown. Increase heat and add curry powder. Fry for 30 seconds. Add salt and vinegar, and cook for 1 minute. Add chicken, and turn so that mixture coats chicken well. Add coconut cream and milk, and simmer gently over a low heat for 20 minutes. Serve with boiled rice.

Facing page: Chicken Curry (top) and Sesame Fried Chicken (bottom).

VEGETABLES AND SAUCES

Asparagus Salad

PREPARATION TIME: 15 minutes

MICROWAVE COOKING TIME:
5-6 minutes

SERVES: 4 people

1lb fresh asparagus
3 tbsps soy sauce
2 tsps sesame oil
1 tbsp sesame seeds

Trim the ends of the asparagus spears, wash and drain well. Cut on the diagonal into 1½ inch lengths, leaving the tips whole. Put into a casserole dish with ½ cup water. Cook, covered, for 5-6 minutes on HIGH. The asparagus should remain crisp. Mix the soy sauce and sesame oil. Drain the asparagus well and toss with the soy sauce mixture. Sprinkle over the sesame seeds and serve hot or cold.

Steamed Eggplant

PREPARATION TIME: 30 minutes

MICROWAVE COOKING TIME:
6-8 minutes

SERVES: 4 people

1 large or 2 small eggplants
1 tbsp sesame oil
3 tbsps rice vinegar or white wine vinegar
3 tbsps light brown sugar
2 tbsps light soy sauce
1 tbsp fresh ginger root, grated
1 clove garlic, minced
Salt

Cut off the stems of the eggplants and then cut them in half, lengthwise. Lightly score the surface of each half and sprinkle with salt. Leave to stand

for 30 minutes. Combine the remaining ingredients in a glass measure. Cook for 1 minute on HIGH to dissolve sugar. Stir well and set aside to allow flavors to blend. Wash the eggplants and dry well. Cut in quarters, lengthwise, and then into 1 inch wedges. Put into a casserole dish with ½ cup water. Cover and cook 5-7 minutes or until just tender. Stir several times during cooking. Drain well. Pour over the sauce and serve hot or cold.

Pea Pods with Water Chestnuts

PREPARATION TIME: 15 minutes

MICROWAVE COOKING TIME:
4 minutes

SERVES: 4 people

8oz pea pods, stems trimmed off
2 tbsps oil
Pinch sugar
Pinch salt
1 small can water chestnuts, sliced in rounds
4 tbsps light stock
1½ tsps cornstarch
Dash sesame oil

Heat a browning dish for 5 minutes on HIGH. Pour in the oil and add the pea pods. Add the salt and sugar and cook 2 minutes on HIGH, stirring frequently. Add the water chestnuts, cover, and set aside while preparing the sauce. Combine the stock and cornstarch in a glass measure. Cook for 2 minutes on HIGH, stirring once, until thickened. Add the sesame oil and mix with the vegetables to serve.

Ginger Dip

PREPARATION TIME: 5 minutes

MAKES: about ½ cup

½ cup wine-flavored vinegar
2 green onions, chopped
1 inch fresh root ginger, peeled and thinly sliced

Mix all the ingredients together and leave for 10-15 minutes before using.

Plum Sauce

PREPARATION TIME: 10 minutes plus soaking overnight

COOKING TIME: 20-25 minutes

MAKES: about 3 cups

1 cup dried apricots
1 cup golden plums, fresh or canned, pitted
⅓ cup raisins
1 inch fresh root ginger, peeled and shredded
1¼ cups brown sugar
4 tbsps vinegar
2-3 dried red chilies
1 tsp salt

Soak apricots overnight in sufficient water to completely cover. Drain apricots and reserve liquid. Mix apricots, plums, raisins, ginger and sugar and add 1 cup reserved apricot liquid. Bring to boil and lower heat to a gentle simmer. Simmer for 10-15

Facing page: Asparagus Salad (top) and Steamed Eggplant (bottom).

This page: Pea Pods with Water Chestnuts (page 142). Facing page: Green Chili and Ginger Dip (top), Garlic Dip (page 148) (center left) and Plum Sauce (page 142) (bottom right).

minutes until it is thick. Add vinegar and coarsely ground chilies to the sauce. Add salt and mix well to blend fruits. Cook for 5-10 minutes until thick and sticky. Cool and bottle.

Green Chili and Ginger Dip

| PREPARATION TIME: 5 minutes |
| MAKES: about ⅓ cup |

4-5 green chilies, chopped
1 inch fresh root ginger, peeled and finely
   sliced
½ tsp salt
½ tsp sugar
⅓ cup vinegar

Mix above ingredients together and allow to stand for 2-3 hours before use.

Szechuan Eggplant

| PREPARATION TIME: 15 minutes |
| COOKING TIME: 18-20 minutes |
| SERVES: 3-4 people |

Salad or olive oil
1 large eggplant, cut into strips 2 inches
   long and ½ inch thick

This page: Bamboo Shoots with Green Vegetables (page 151) (top right), Sweet and Sour Cabbage (page 148) (center left) and Szechuan Eggplant (page 144) (bottom). Facing page: Sweet-Sour Cabbage.

1 cup cooked and shredded chicken
1 red or green chili, cut into strips

SEASONING
1 cup chicken broth
1 tsp fine granulated sugar
1½ tsps wine-flavored vinegar
½ tsp salt
½ tsp freshly ground black pepper

SAUCE
1½ tsps cornstarch
1½ tbsps water
1 tsp sesame oil

Heat the wok and add 3 tbsps oil. Add the eggplant and stir-fry for 4-5 minutes. The eggplant absorbs a lot of oil; keep stirring or else it will burn. Remove from wok and keep on one side. Heat the wok and add 2 tbsps oil. Add the garlic and ginger and fry for 1 minute. Add the onions and fry for 2 minutes. Add the chicken and chili. Cook for 1 minute. Return the eggplant to the wok. Add the blended seasoning ingredients and simmer for 6-7 minutes. Stir in the blended sauce ingredients and simmer until the sauce thickens. Serve with extra sesame oil if desired. This dish goes well with Yung Chow fried rice or rice supreme.

Sweet-Sour Cabbage

PREPARATION TIME: 20 minutes

MICROWAVE COOKING TIME: 11-13 minutes

SERVES: 4 people

1 medium head white cabbage, about 2lbs
1 small red chili pepper (use less if desired)
½ cup light brown sugar
⅓ cup rice vinegar
2 tbsps light soy sauce
Salt
3 tbsps oil

3 cloves garlic, peeled and finely sliced
1 inch fresh root ginger, peeled and shredded
1 onion, peeled and finely chopped
2 green onions, chopped

Cut the cabbage into ½ inch slices, discarding the core. Cut the chili pepper into thin, short strips, discarding the seeds. Mix all the ingredients together except the oil. Pour the oil into a large bowl and heat for 2 minutes on HIGH. Add the cabbage and the liquid and cover the bowl with pierced plastic wrap.

Cook on HIGH for 9-11 minutes. Allow to cool in the bowl, stirring frequently. When cold, refrigerate. Keeps several days.

Sweet and Sour Cabbage

| **PREPARATION TIME:** 10 minutes |
| **COOKING TIME:** 10 minutes |
| **SERVES:** 4 people |

1lb white cabbage, shredded
½ tsp baking soda
1 tsp salt
2 tsps fine granulated sugar
1 tbsp salad or olive oil

SAUCE
2½ tbsps fine granulated sugar
2½ tbsps wine-flavored vinegar
1 cup chicken broth or water
Pinch salt
1¼ tbsps cornstarch
Few drops red food coloring
1 tsp ketchup

Boil the cabbage in a large pan of water with the baking soda, salt, and sugar for 2-3 minutes. Drain the cabbage and discard the boiling water. Keep the cabbage in cold water for 5 minutes. Drain and keep on one side. Heat the wok and add the oil. Fry the cabbage until it is heated through. Remove onto a serving dish. Add the well-stirred sauce ingredients to the wok and gently bring to the boil, stirring. Stir over the heat until the sauce thickens. Pour over the cabbage and serve immediately.

Chili Oil Dip

| **PREPARATION TIME:** 5-8 minutes |
| **COOKING TIME:** 5 minutes |
| **MAKES:** about ⅓ cup |

¼ cup salad or olive oil
2 cloves of garlic, minced
3-4 coarsely ground dry red chilies
2 tbsps sesame oil

Heat the oil and fry garlic till dark brown. Add chilies and fry for a few seconds. Add sesame oil and remove from heat. Stir well and cool.

Garlic Dip

| **PREPARATION TIME:** 5 minutes |
| **MAKES:** about ⅓ cup |

⅓ cup wine-flavored vinegar
2 tbsps minced garlic
Pinch fine granulated sugar

Mix all the ingredients together and leave for 2 hours before using.

Soy Dip

| **PREPARATION TIME:** 5 minutes |
| **MAKES:** about ⅓ cup |

¼ cup light soy sauce
1 tbsp dark soy sauce

Facing page left: Sweet and Sour Sauce (page 160) (top), Soy Dip (center) and Chili Oil Dip (bottom). Facing page right: Hoi Sin Sauce (top), Chili Sauce (center) and Ginger Dip (page 142) (bottom). This page: Lettuce and Bean Sprouts with Soy Sauce (left), Braised Eggplant and Chicken with Chili (page 150) (center) and Braised Cauliflower with Chili (page 151) (right).

½ tsp fine granulated sugar
2-3 green chilies, chopped
2-3 slices fresh root ginger, minced

Mix the above ingredients together and allow to stand for 10-15 minutes before using. Keep in an airtight glass jar.

Hoi Sin Sauce

PREPARATION TIME: 5 minutes
COOKING TIME: 8 minutes
MAKES: about 2 cups

This can be bought ready-made; the home-made variety does not have quite the same flavor.

1 tbsp dark soy bean paste
2 cloves garlic, minced
1 tbsp fine granulated sugar
½ tsp salt
1 tsp all-purpose flour
½ tsp chili powder
1¾ cups wine-flavored vinegar

Mix all the above ingredients together in a pan and bring to the boil. Simmer gently for 5-6 minutes or until it thickens. Cool and bottle.

Chili Sauce

PREPARATION TIME: 5 minutes
COOKING TIME: 5 minutes
MAKES: about 1½ cups

¼ cup dried red chilies, coarsely ground
¼ cup dried apricots, chopped

1 cup wine-flavored vinegar
1 tsp salt
1 tsp fine granulated sugar
1 tsp cornstarch

Mix all the above ingredients together in a pan and bring to the boil. Simmer gently for 5 minutes until the sauce thickens. Cool and serve. Will keep bottled for a few weeks.

Lettuce and Bean Sprouts with Soy Sauce

PREPARATION TIME: 15 minutes
COOKING TIME: 5 minutes
SERVES: 4 people

1½ cups bean sprouts (moong or soya)
8oz lettuce
1 tbsp salad or olive oil
1 inch fresh root ginger, peeled and shredded
1 green or red chili, seeded and split in half

This page: Pineapple Sauce. Facing page: Mixed Vegetables with Peanut Sauce.

Salt and freshly ground black pepper

SAUCE
3 tbsps light soy sauce
2 tsps dark soy sauce
1½ tbsps medium white wine or rice wine
½ tsp fine granulated sugar
Salt and freshly ground black pepper to
   taste
½ tsp sesame oil

Trim the bean sprouts by pinching off the grey and brown ends, as they impart a bitter taste to the dish. Pick off bean seed skin if using soya beans. Cut soya bean sprouts in 2-3 pieces. Rinse in cold water and drain. Wash and drain lettuce before shredding into 2 inch pieces. Heat the oil in the wok and stir-fry the ginger and chili for 1 minute. Add the lettuce and toss for 1 minute. Drain and remove on to a plate. Place the bean sprouts in a colander and pour boiling water over them. Drain thoroughly and add to the lettuce. Sprinkle with salt and pepper and keep covered. Mix the sauce ingredients together in the wok. Stir over the heat until blended. Pour this sauce over the vegetables and serve immediately.

Pineapple Sauce

PREPARATION TIME: 10-15 minutes

MICROWAVE COOKING TIME:
4 minutes

MAKES: About 2 cups

8oz can crushed pineapple, or 1 fresh
   pineapple, peeled and cored
1½ tsp cornstarch dissolved in 1 tbsp water
1 tbsp light soy sauce
1½ tsp sugar
1 tbsp white wine
1 piece ginger root, grated
Pinch salt

If using fresh pineapple, work in a food processor until finely chopped. Add remaining ingredients and mix well in a small, deep bowl. Cook 4 minutes on HIGH until the sauce thickens and clears. Serve with duck or shrimp.

Braised Eggplant and Chicken with Chili

PREPARATION TIME: 10 minutes

COOKING TIME: about 15 minutes

SERVES: 4 people

⅓ cup salad or olive oil
2 cloves of garlic, peeled and sliced
1lb eggplant, cut into 2x2½ inch pieces

1 tbsp soy bean paste (or canned red
   kidney beans, made into paste)
½ tsp ground dry chili or chili powder
Salt
1¾ cups chicken broth
1 inch fresh root ginger, peeled and sliced
2-3 green onions, chopped
2 cups chicken, shredded (cooked or
   uncooked)

SEASONING
2 tbsps light soy sauce
½ tsp fine granulated sugar
1½ tbsps cornstarch
3 tbsps broth or water

Heat 4 tbsps oil in the wok and stir-fry the garlic for 2 minutes. Add the eggplant, which will soak up all the oil. Stir-fry for 3-4 minutes, stirring constantly to avoid burning. Add the bean paste, chili powder, and salt to taste and mix well. Add the chicken broth. Cover and cook for 4-6 minutes, simmering gently. Remove the eggplant and arrange on a dish. Save the sauce. Clean the wok and heat the remaining oil. Stir-fry the ginger for 1 minute. Add the onions and chicken and stir-fry for 2 minutes. Add the blended seasoning ingredients and the reserved eggplant sauce and simmer gently until it thickens. Pour over the eggplant and serve immediately.

Mixed Vegetables with Peanut Sauce

PREPARATION TIME: 20 minutes

COOKING TIME: 30 minutes

SERVES: 4 people as a vegetable

1 cup bean-sprouts
1 cup Chinese cabbage, shredded
½ cup green beans, trimmed
Half a cucumber, cut into 2" strips
1 carrot, peeled and cut into thin strips
1 potato, peeled and cut into thin strips
1 tbsp peanut oil

PEANUT SAUCE
2 tbsps peanut oil
⅔ cup raw shelled peanuts
2 red chili peppers, seeds removed, and
   chopped finely, or 1 tsp chili powder
2 shallots, peeled and chopped finely

on paper towels. Blend or pound chili peppers, shallots and garlic to a smooth paste. Grind or blend peanuts to a powder. Heat oil and fry chili paste for 2 minutes. Add water, and bring to the boil. Add peanuts, brown sugar, lemon juice, and salt to taste. Stir until sauce is thick – about 10 minutes – and add coconut milk. Garnish vegetable dish with slices of hard-boiled egg, and cucumber and serve with peanut sauce.

Braised Cauliflower with Chili

PREPARATION TIME:	5 minutes
COOKING TIME:	10 minutes
SERVES:	4 people

4 tbsps salad or olive oil
1 inch fresh root ginger, peeled and thinly
  sliced
1 small cauliflower, cut into 1 inch
  flowerets
2-3 green or red chilies, sliced into
  quarters and seeded
3 green onions
Salt to taste
1 tsp fine granulated sugar
1¼ cups chicken broth
1½ tsps cornstarch
1½ tbsps water

Heat the wok and add the oil. Stir-fry the ginger for 1 minute. Reduce the heat and add the cauliflower and chilies. Stir-fry for 3-4 minutes. Add the green onions, season with salt and sprinkle with sugar. Mix for 1 minute and then add the broth. Cover and cook for 2 minutes. Add the blended cornstarch and water and stir over the heat until the sauce has thickened.

Bamboo Shoots with Green Vegetables

PREPARATION TIME:	10 minutes
COOKING TIME:	10-12 minutes
SERVES:	4 people

Salad or olive oil for cooking
8oz spinach, or chopped broccoli

---

1 clove garlic, crushed
1 tsp brown sugar
Juice of half a lemon
¼ cup coconut milk
⅔ cup water
Salt

GARNISH
Sliced hard-boiled eggs
Sliced cucumber

Heat wok and add 1 tbsp peanut oil. When hot, toss in carrot and potato. Stir-fry for 2 minutes and add green beans and cabbage. Cook for a further 3 minutes. Add bean-sprouts and cucumber, and stir-fry for 2 minutes. Place in a serving dish. Make peanut sauce. Heat wok, add 2 tbsps peanut oil, and fry peanuts for 2-3 minutes. Remove and drain

SEASONING
½ cup chicken broth or water
¼ tsp monosodium glutamate (optional)
¼ tsp salt
¼ tsp fine granulated sugar

1 cup bamboo shoots, sliced

SAUCE
1½ tsps light soy sauce
Pinch monosodium glutamate
1½ tsps cornstarch
3 tsps water
1 tbsp cooked oil

Heat 2 tbsps oil in the wok. Fry the spinach for 2 minutes and add the mixed seasoning ingredients. Simmer for 1 minute and remove from the wok onto a dish. Heat the wok and add 1 tbsp oil. Add the bamboo shoots and fry for 1-2 minutes. Return the spinach mixture to the wok. Cook for 3 minutes. Mix together the ingredients for thickening the sauce. Add to the wok and cook for 1-2 minutes. Serve with roast Peking duck, or as a side dish.

Hot Mustard Sauce

PREPARATION TIME: 10 minutes

MICROWAVE COOKING TIME:
4 minutes

MAKES: About 3-4 cups

4 tbsps dry mustard

This page: Hot Mustard Sauce. Facing page: Stir-Fried Vegetable Medley (page 157) (top) and Sweet and Sour Cabbage (page 148) (bottom).

4 tbsps rice wine vinegar
1½ tsps cornstarch
½ cup water
3 tbsps honey
Salt

Mix the mustard and cornstarch together. Beat in the water, vinegar and honey gradually until smooth. Add a small pinch of salt and cook, uncovered, in a small, deep bowl for 4 minutes on HIGH. Stir every 30 seconds until thickened. Serve with appetizers or seafood.

Add the tree ears, cover the dish and leave to stand while preparing the sauce. Mix the remaining ingredients except the sesame oil in a glass measure. Cook for 2 minutes on HIGH, stirring once until thickened. Combine with the vegetables and stir in the sesame oil to serve.

Wok Sweet and Sour Cabbage

PREPARATION TIME: 5 minutes

COOKING TIME: 20 minutes

SERVES: 4 people as a vegetable

Half a small cabbage
2 tbsps butter or margarine
3 tbsps vinegar
2 tbsps sugar
3 tbsps water
Salt
Pepper

Slice cabbage into shreds. Melt butter in wok. Put cabbage into wok with other ingredients and set over a moderate heat. Stir until hot, then cover and simmer for 15 minutes. Adjust seasoning if necessary. Serve hot.

Spicy Cucumbers

PREPARATION TIME: 30 minutes

MICROWAVE COOKING TIME: 2 minutes

SERVES: 4 people

1 large cucumber
Salt
3 tbsps light soy sauce
Pinch five-spice powder
¼ tsp crushed red pepper
2 tsp sesame oil
1 tbsp rice vinegar
3 tbsps Chinese parsley leaves

Peel thin strips off the cucumber for a white and green stripe effect. Cut in

Beans with Tree Ears and Bamboo Shoots

PREPARATION TIME: 30 minutes

MICROWAVE COOKING TIME: 4 minutes

SERVES: 4 people

6 pieces Chinese black fungi (tree or
*   wood ears), soaked 30 minutes*
8oz green beans, cut into 2 inch diagonal
*   pieces*

2 whole pieces canned bamboo shoots,
*   cut into thin triangular pieces*
2 tbsps oil
2 tbsps soy sauce
2 tsps cornstarch
4 tbsps light stock and wine mixed
Dash sesame oil
Salt and pepper

Heat a browning dish for 5 minutes on HIGH. Pour in the oil and add the beans and bamboo shoots. Cook, uncovered, for 2 minutes on HIGH.

This page: Spinach, Chinese Style (page 157) (top) and Spicy Cucumbers (bottom). Facing page: Beans with Tree Ears and Bamboo Shoots.

the ginger and cook, uncovered, for 2 minutes on HIGH, stirring frequently. Add the flowerets, cover and set aside while preparing the sauce. Combine the remaining ingredients in a glass measure. Cook, uncovered, for 5-6 minutes on HIGH until thickened. Pour over the broccoli and stir together to serve.

Ginger Sauce

PREPARATION TIME: 5 minutes

COOKING TIME: 10 minutes

1 tbsp grated ginger root
2 tbsps light soy sauce
1 tbsp Chinese wine, or dry sherry
1 tsp sugar
1 tsp cornstarch
2 tbsps water
1 tbsp oil

Heat wok, add oil and gently fry ginger. Mix together soy sauce, wine and sugar. Blend cornstarch with water, and add to soy/wine mixture. Pour into wok and bring to the boil. Simmer for 3 minutes, stirring continuously. Push through strainer. Good with sea-food, pork, beef and crab rolls.

Special Fried Rice

PREPARATION TIME: 15 minutes

COOKING TIME: 20 minutes

SERVES: 4 people

2 cups boiled rice
4oz shrimp, shelled and de-veined
8oz Chinese barbecued pork, or cooked ham, diced or cut into small pieces
1 cup bean-sprouts
½ cup frozen peas
2 green onions, sliced diagonally
1 tbsp light soy sauce
1 tsp dark soy sauce
2 tbsps peanut oil
Salt
Pepper

PANCAKE
2 eggs, beaten
Salt

half lengthwise, or in quarters if the cucumber is thick. Cut the lengths into 2 inch pieces. Sprinkle with salt and leave to stand 30 minutes. Wash and dry well. Combine the cucumber with all the remaining ingredients except the parsley in a deep bowl. Partially cover and cook for 2 minutes on HIGH. Add the parsley and leave in the bowl to cool. When cold, refrigerate. Serve on the same day.

Ginger Broccoli

PREPARATION TIME: 20 minutes

MICROWAVE COOKING TIME:
7-8 minutes

SERVES: 4 people

1½ lbs broccoli
2 tbsps oil
3 inch piece fresh ginger root, peeled and very finely shredded
Pinch salt
Pinch sugar
1 tsp cornstarch
½ cup light stock
Dash light soy sauce

Heat a browning dish for 5 minutes on HIGH. Cut off the tough ends of the broccoli stems. Cut the flowerets from the stems in small clusters. Peel the stems with a vegetable peeler and cut them into thin diagonal slices. Pour the oil into the browning dish and add the broccoli stem slices. Add

2 minutes. With a slotted spoon, remove and set aside. Re-heat oil and add rice. Stir continuously over a low heat until rice is heated through. Add soy sauces and mix well. Add peas, green onions, bean-sprouts, meat, shrimp, and salt and pepper to taste. Mix thoroughly. Serve hot, garnished with pancake and green onion flowers. The pancake may be sliced very finely and mixed in if desired.

Spinach, Chinese Style

PREPARATION TIME: 15 minutes
MICROWAVE COOKING TIME: 2 minutes plus 1 minute standing time
SERVES: 4 people

1½ lbs fresh spinach, stalks removed
2 tbsps oil
Salt
Sugar
Soy sauce
2 green onions, white part only, finely
    sliced

Wash the spinach well and pat the leaves dry. Heat a browning dish for 4 minutes on HIGH. Pour in the oil and add the spinach. Add a pinch of salt and sugar and cook, uncovered, for 2 minutes on HIGH, stirring frequently. Add the green onions and a dash of soy sauce. Leave to stand 1 minute before serving.

Stir-Fried Vegetable Medley

PREPARATION TIME: 20 minutes
COOKING TIME: 10 minutes
SERVES: 4 people as a vegetable

2 carrots, cut into flowers (slice strips out
    lengthwise to produce flowers when cut
    across into rounds)

GARNISH
2 green onion flowers (trim green onions, slice lengthwise, leaving one end intact and leave in cold water in refrigerator until curling).

Heat wok and add 1 tbsp of peanut oil. Roll oil around surface. Make pancake by mixing beaten eggs with a pinch of salt and 1 tsp of oil. Add egg mixture to wok, and move wok back and forth so that the mixture spreads over the surface. When lightly browned on the underside, turn over and cook on other side. Set aside to cool. Heat remaining oil in wok. When hot, add green onions and peas and cook, covered, for

Facing page: Ginger Broccoli. This page: Special Fried Rice (top) and Ginger Sauce (bottom).

1 can baby corn, drained
2 cups broccoli flowerets (slit stems to
    ensure quick cooking)
1 onion, peeled and sliced in julienne
    strips
2 sticks celery, with tough strings removed,
    sliced diagonally in half-moon shapes
1 zucchini, sliced diagonally
1 clove garlic, crushed
1 tbsp light soy sauce
¼ tsp finely-grated ginger
2 tbsps oil
Salt
Pepper

This page: Yang Chow Fried Rice (top
right) and Plain Fried Rice (page 43)
(bottom left). Facing page: Ten Varieties
of Beauty (page 160).

Prepare all ingredients before starting
to cook. Heat wok and add oil. Add
ginger, garlic, onion, carrots, broccoli
and zucchini, and toss in oil for 2-3
minutes. Add celery and baby corn,
and toss 1-2 minutes longer. Season
with soy sauce, and salt and pepper if
desired. Add cornstarch to thicken
vegetable juices if necessary.

Yang Chow Fried Rice

PREPARATION TIME:	10 minutes
COOKING TIME:	6-8 minutes
SERVES:	6 people

3 tbsps salad or olive oil
1 egg, beaten
1 cup cooked meat, chopped (pork, lamb,
    beef)
1 cup medium shrimp, shelled and
    chopped
½ cup shelled green peas, lightly cooked
2 green onions, chopped

1lb dry, cooked rice
Salt to taste
1 tsp monosodium glutamate (optional)

Heat 1 tbsp oil in a wok. Fry the beaten egg until set, and break into small lumps. Remove the egg. Add the remaining oil and fry the meat, shrimp, peas and onions for 1-2 minutes. Add the cooked rice and sprinkle with salt and monosodium glutamate. Fry for 3 minutes. Mix in the cooked egg and serve immediately.

Mango Sauce

PREPARATION TIME: 5 minutes

COOKING TIME: 20 minutes

1 can sliced mangoes
⅔ cup malt vinegar
½ tsp garam masala
1 tsp grated ginger root
1 tbsp sugar
1 tsp oil
Salt

Heat wok and add oil. Add garam masala and ginger, and cook for 1 minute. Add undrained mangoes, vinegar and sugar, and salt to taste. Simmer, uncovered, for 15 minutes. Blend and push through a strainer. Good with chicken, beef and spring rolls (egg rolls).

Ten Varieties of Beauty

PREPARATION TIME: 20 minutes

MICROWAVE COOKING TIME: 6-8 minutes

SERVES: 4-6 people

4 tbsps oil
3 sticks celery, diagonally sliced
2 carrots, peeled and cut into ribbons with a vegetable peeler
3oz pea pods
1 red pepper, thickly sliced
4 green onions, diagonally sliced
8 ears of baby corn
2oz bean sprouts
10 water chestnuts, sliced

½ small can sliced bamboo shoots
10 Chinese dried mushrooms, soaked in hot water, stalks removed
1 cup chicken stock
2 tbsps cornstarch
3 tbsps light soy sauce
Sesame oil

Heat a browning dish for 5 minutes on HIGH. Pour in the oil and add the celery and carrots. Cook for 1 minute on HIGH. Remove from the dish and add the pea pods, red pepper and corn. Cook for 1 minute on HIGH and place with the celery and carrots. Add the onions, bean sprouts, water chestnuts and bamboo shoots to the dish. Cook for 1 minute on HIGH, adding the mushrooms after 30 seconds. Place with the rest of vegetables. Combine the rest of the ingredients in a glass measure. Cook 2-3 minutes on HIGH until thickened. Taste and add salt if necessary. Pour over the vegetables and stir carefully. Reheat for 1-2 minutes on HIGH before serving.

Julienne of Vegetables

PREPARATION TIME: 20 minutes

COOKING TIME: 15 minutes

SERVES: 4 people as a vegetable

2 medium onions, peeled and cut into matchstick strips
2 carrots, scraped and cut into matchstick strips
1 parsnip, scraped and cut into matchstick strips
2 sticks celery, cut into matchstick strips
1 turnip, peeled and cut into matchstick strips
1 tbsp oil
2 tbsps water
1 tbsp butter
Salt
Pepper

Prepare vegetables. Heat wok and add oil. Stir-fry vegetable strips over gentle heat for 5 minutes. Add water and salt to taste, and increase heat. Cook for a further 5 minutes over high heat. Drain any liquid from wok. Add butter and freshly-ground black pepper, and toss to coat well.

Sweet and Sour Sauce

PREPARATION TIME: 10 minutes

COOKING TIME: 10 minutes

Juice of 2 oranges
2 tbsps lemon juice
2 tbsps white wine vinegar
1 tbsp sugar
1 tbsp tomato paste
1 tbsp light soy sauce
½ tsp salt
1 tbsp cornstarch
2 tbsps water
Drop of red food coloring if desired

Combine orange and lemon juice, sugar, vinegar, tomato paste, soy sauce, salt, and red coloring (if desired). Place in wok and heat gently. Blend cornstarch with water, and stir into sauce. Bring to boil and simmer for 3 minutes, stirring continuously. Good with fish, pork, wontons and spring rolls (egg rolls).

Ratatouille

PREPARATION TIME: 30 minutes

COOKING TIME: 30 minutes

SERVES: 4 people as a vegetable

1 eggplant, sliced into 1″ slices
2 zucchini, sliced diagonally
4 tomatoes, chopped roughly
2 onions, peeled and quartered
1 red pepper, cored, seeds removed, and chopped roughly
1 green pepper, cored, seeds removed, and chopped roughly
3 cloves garlic, crushed
1 tsp dry basil
¼ cup olive oil
Salt
Pepper

Slice eggplant and sprinkle with salt. Leave for 20 minutes. Rinse in water, and dry on paper towels. Chop roughly. Heat wok and add oil. Add onions, garlic and basil. Cover and cook gently until onion is soft but not colored. Add peppers, zucchini and eggplant. Cover and fry gently for 15 minutes stirring occasionally. Add tomatoes and salt and pepper to taste and cook covered for a further 10 minutes. Serve hot or chilled.

for 1 minute. Drain the mushrooms and discard the water. Mix the seasoning ingredients together and marinate all the mushrooms for 5-6 minutes. Discard marinade. Bring 5 cups of water to the boil and add the baking soda and salt. Blanch the greens for 2 minutes. Drain the greens. Discard water. Sprinkle ½ tsp salt over the bean curd. Deep-fry in hot oil until golden brown. Drain and remove. Heat 2 tbsps oil in the wok and stir-fry the ginger, onions and ham for 2-3 minutes. Return the mushrooms to the wok and mix with the ginger and onions. Add the blended sauce ingredients and bring to boil. Add the bean curd and simmer until the sauce thickens. Arrange the greens on a dish and pour the sauce over them. Sprinkle with freshly ground black pepper.

Okra and Tomatoes

PREPARATION TIME: 15 minutes

COOKING TIME: 10 minutes

SERVES: 4 people as a vegetable

8oz okra, sliced into ½" pieces
1 onion, peeled and chopped
2 tomatoes, chopped
1 red chili pepper, seeds removed, and
    sliced finely
¼ tsp turmeric
¼ tsp chili powder
½ tsp garam masala
1 tbsp oil or ghee
⅔ cup water
Salt

Heat wok and add oil or ghee. When hot, add turmeric, chili powder and garam masala, and fry for 30 seconds. Add onion, okra and red chili pepper, and stir-fry for 3 minutes. Add tomatoes, water, and salt to taste, and cook uncovered for 5 minutes or until sauce thickens.

Fried Vegetables with Ginger

PREPARATION TIME: 10 minutes

COOKING TIME: 13-15 minutes

SERVES: 6 people

Fried Bean Curd with Mushrooms

PREPARATION TIME: 15 minutes

COOKING TIME: 12-15 minutes

SERVES: 4 people

8oz large cap mushrooms, sliced

SEASONING
1 tbsp rice wine or dry sherry
2 tsps fine granulated sugar

4 dried Chinese mushrooms, soaked and
    sliced
Pinch baking soda
8oz mustard green or spinach, cut into 3
    inch pieces

Above: Okra and Tomatoes.

4 squares bean curd (tofu), cubed
Salad or olive oil
1 inch fresh root ginger, peeled and
    shredded
2 green onions, chopped
½ cup cooked ham, shredded

SAUCE
1½ tbsps oyster sauce
1½ tsps dark soy sauce
1½ tbsps cornstarch
6 tbsps broth or water
Freshly ground black pepper

Blanch the fresh mushrooms in water

Inset left: Fried Vegetables with Ginger (page 161) (top right) and Fried Bean Curd with Mushrooms (page 161) (bottom). Ratatouille (page 160) (right) and Julienne of Vegetables (page 160) (bottom right).

2¼lbs mixed Chinese green vegetables (cabbage, spinach, kale, broccoli, Chinese leaf etc.)
½ cup pea pods
1 tsp baking soda
2 tsps fine granulated sugar
1 tsp salt
1 tbsp cooked oil
4 tbsps salad or olive oil
1 inch fresh root ginger, peeled and shredded
1 green pepper, seeded and diced
1 green or red chili, sliced into strips

SAUCE
2 tsps dark soy sauce
1 tsp fine granulated sugar
1 cup chicken broth
2 tsps cornstarch
1 tsp five spice powder

TO SERVE
½ tsp sesame oil
Freshly ground black pepper to taste

Cut the green vegetables into 3 inch pieces. Bring a large pan of water to the boil and add the seasoning ingredients. Add the pea pods and greens and cook for 4-5 minutes. Drain green vegetables and discard water. Add 1 tbsp oil to the vegetables and keep covered. Heat the remaining oil in the wok and stir-fry the ginger for 1 minute. Add the green pepper and chilies and stir-fry for 1-2 minutes. Add the blended sauce ingredients and stir well. Simmer gently for 3-4 minutes. Add the green vegetables and cook for 1 minute. Serve immediately, sprinkled with sesame oil and pepper.

DESSERTS

Almond Cookies

PREPARATION TIME: 20 minutes

COOKING TIME: 12-15 minutes

MAKES: 60 cookies

1 generous cup shortening
½ cup fine granulated sugar
⅓ cup brown sugar
1 egg, beaten
Few drops almond extract
2¼ cups all-purpose flour
Pinch salt
1½ tsps baking powder
½ cup blanched almonds
1 egg yolk
2 tbsps water

Cream the shortening with the sugars until light and fluffy. Add the egg and almond extract and beat until smooth. Sift the flour, salt and baking powder. Mix the dry ingredients into the creamed mixture. Shape into small balls on a lightly floured surface. Flatten slightly and press an almond into the center of each one. Place onto a greased cookie sheet. Mix the egg yolk with the water. Brush the cookies with the egg glaze. Bake at 350°F for 12-15 minutes.

Sweet Dumplings

PREPARATION TIME: 10 minutes

COOKING TIME: 15-20 minutes

MAKES: 10-12

Salad or olive oil
½ cup fine granulated sugar
⅓ cup plain red bean paste
⅓ cup desiccated coconut
4 egg whites
1½ tbsps all-purpose flour
4 tbsps cornstarch
Confectioner's sugar

Heat 1 tbsp oil in a wok and add the sugar, bean paste and coconut. Stir-fry for 4-5 minutes until the sugar melts and the paste is smooth and shiny. Fry for a few minutes more and then allow to cool on a dish. Whip the egg whites until stiff and mix with the flour and cornstarch to a smooth batter. Beat well. Clean the wok and heat sufficient oil for deep frying. Make 10-12 even-sized balls from the bean paste mixture. Dip each ball into the batter and then deep fry for 3-4 minutes until golden and crisp. Fry a few at a time and drain on kitchen paper. Dust with sifted confectioner's sugar before serving.

Steamed Custard

PREPARATION TIME: 10 minutes

COOKING TIME: 20 minutes

1⅔ cups milk
2 tbsps sugar
2 eggs, beaten
½ tsp vanilla extract
Sprinkling of ground nutmeg or cinnamon

Place sugar and milk in wok. Heat gently until the milk reaches a low simmer and the sugar has dissolved. Remove from wok and leave to cool for 5 minutes. Meanwhile, wash wok and place steaming rack inside, with 1½"-2" of hot water. Return to heat and bring water to simmering point. Pour milk and sugar mixture over beaten eggs. Beat again, and add the vanilla extract, stirring well. Pour mixture into a heat-proof dish or metal molds and sprinkle lightly with nutmeg or cinnamon. Place on rack and cover with waxed paper, so condensation does not drop into custard. Cover wok and steam for 10-15 minutes. To test if cooked, a knife inserted in center will come out clean, and custard will be set and gelatinous. Cover and cool for 1 hour, then place in refrigerator until needed.

Bananas Cooked in Coconut Milk

PREPARATION TIME: 20 minutes

COOKING TIME: 20 minutes

SERVES: 4 people

4-6 large, ripe bananas, peeled and sliced
diagonally into 3 or 4 pieces
1 tbsp brown sugar
1 cup desiccated coconut
⅔ cup milk

GARNISH
Desiccated coconut

Put sugar, coconut and milk into wok, and bring to simmering point. Turn off heat and allow to cool for 15 minutes. Push through strainer or a piece of cheesecloth to squeeze out juices. Return to wok, and simmer for 10 minutes, or until creamy. Add bananas, and cook slowly until bananas are soft. Serve immediately sprinkled with desiccated coconut.

Facing page: Sweet Dumplings (top) and Almond Cookies (center left).

Red Bean Filled Dim Sums

PREPARATION TIME: 45-50 minutes

COOKING TIME: 10-12 minutes

MAKES: about 24

¼ cup fine granulated sugar
1¼ cups warm water
1¼ tbsps dry yeast
3¾ cups all-purpose flour
2 tbsps melted shortening
1 egg white, beaten

FILLING
¾-1 cup sweet bean paste
Red food coloring

Dissolve the sugar in the warm water and add the yeast. Stir until dissolved. Leave in a warm place until frothy. Sift the flour into a mixing bowl and add the melted shortening and the yeast mixture. Mix together. Turn the mixture onto a floured surface and knead to a smooth and elastic dough. Roll into a long sausage and divide into 24 equal portions. Roll each portion into a 2 inch flat circle. Brush edges of dough with beaten egg white. Place 1 tbsp of filling into the center of each circle and pull the dough around it to enclose the filling. Pleat the open edges in a circular fashion, so that a small opening is left in the middle of the pleating. Place a small piece of greased foil over the pleats on each dim sum. Leave for 10-12 minutes until the dough becomes springy to the touch. Put a dab of red food coloring on each dim sum. Arrange the dim sums in a bamboo steaming basket and steam over boiling water for 10-12 minutes. The dim sums are ready when they are dry and smooth. Alternatively they can be baked at 350°F for about 20 minutes.

Chinese Bean Buns

PREPARATION TIME: about 2 hours, including proving time

COOKING TIME: about 30 minutes

MAKES: about 14

¼ cup milk
⅓ cup fine granulated sugar
½ tsp salt
1½ tbsps shortening
¼ cup warm water
2 tsps dry yeast
1 egg, beaten
2¼ cups all-purpose flour

Bring the milk almost to the boil. Stir in the sugar, salt and shortening. Cool slightly. Put the warm water and yeast into a bowl and stir to mix. Add the lukewarm milk mixture. Add the beaten egg and 1 cup of the flour and beat until smooth. Add the remaining flour and mix to a dough. Turn dough out onto a well-floured board and knead until smooth and elastic. Place in a greased bowl. Brush the dough with oil and cover. Leave to rise in a warm place until doubled in size (about 1 hour).

FILLING
⅓ cup sweet bean paste
2 tbsps fine granulated sugar
2 tbsps chopped walnuts
1 tbsp shortening

Heat the filling ingredients together in a wok for 5-6 minutes until smooth and shiny. Remove and cool. Divide the filling into 12-14 portions. Knead the risen dough again for 2 minutes and then divide the dough into 12-14 portions. Flatten into thick, circular shapes 4 inches in diameter. Place a chopstick on each circle of dough to mark it in half, and then in half again. Cut along the marks to within ⅓ of the center. Place one portion of filling in the center of the dough circle and fold the cut ends in to meet in the center, to form a rosette. Secure by pinching ends of dough together. Place a piece of greased foil over the pinched ends and place the buns on a greased baking tray. Brush with a little milk. Bake at 375°F for 20-25 minutes.

This page: Chinese Bean Buns (top left) and Red Bean Filled Dim Sums (right). Facing page: Steamed Custard (page 164) (top) and Bananas Cooked in Coconut Milk (page 164) (bottom).

3 cups canned lychees, stones removed
4-5 rings canned pineapple
Few drops vanilla or almond extract

Drain the lychees into a bowl, reserving the juice. Slice each pineapple ring into ½ inch long strips. Press one or two strips of pineapple into each lychee. Arrange the pineapple-filled lychees in a deep serving dish. Mix the pineapple and lychee liquid with a few drops of essence. Spoon over the stuffed fruits. Serve well chilled. Alternatively, stuff the lychees with maraschino cherries, mango, canned pears, oranges etc.

Sweet Almond Pudding

PREPARATION TIME: 4-5 minutes

COOKING TIME: 6 minutes

SERVES: 4-6 people

1 cup blanched almonds
1¾ cups water
¾ cup fine granulated sugar
4 tbsps rice powder, or ground rice
⅔ cup milk

Blend the blanched almonds and water in the blender. Put into a pan and bring to the boil. Add the sugar and stir over the heat until the sugar has dissolved. Add the rice slowly to the milk and stir gradually into the simmering sugar and almond mixture. Cook gently until the mixture thickens. Remove from the heat and pour into a serving dish. Serve hot or cold.

Agar-Agar Pudding

PREPARATION TIME: 5 minutes

COOKING TIME: 4-5 minutes

SERVES: 4 people

2½ cups milk
½ cup fine granulated sugar
2 tbsps ground almonds
4 tbsps agar-agar (also called Chinese grass)
2 tbsps blanched and chopped almonds

Mix the milk, sugar and ground almonds together in a pan and stir over the heat for 4 minutes. Add the agar-agar and stir until dissolved. Stir in the

Jade Pieces

PREPARATION TIME: 1 hour

MICROWAVE COOKING TIME: 43-49 minutes

MAKES: 24 pieces (approx.)

1 lb green split peas, soaked overnight, or brought to the boil, cooked 10 minutes on HIGH and left to stand for 1 hour
½ cup sugar
3 cups water
4 tbsps cornstarch
1 piece preserved ginger, finely chopped
3 tbsps desiccated coconut
Few drops green food coloring

Drain the peas and return them to a large glass bowl. Add the water, loosely cover the bowl and cook on HIGH for 40-45 minutes, or until the peas are very soft. Purée the peas with the sugar and food coloring. Mix the cornstarch with a little water and add to the peas. Return to the bowl and cook, uncovered, 3-4 minutes until cornstarch thickens. Add the ginger and pour into a shallow dish to the depth of 1 inch. Sprinkle the coconut over the surface and chill until firm. Cut into diamond shapes to serve.

Stuffed Lychees

PREPARATION TIME: 20 minutes

SERVES: 6 people

chopped almonds. Pour into a shallow dish 1 inch deep. Cool and keep in refrigerator until set. Serve chilled, cut into diamond or square shapes.

Date and Red Bean Winter Pudding

PREPARATION TIME: 20 minutes
MICROWAVE COOKING TIME: 17-22 minutes plus 3 minutes standing time
SERVES: 4 people

1lb dried, stoned dates
3 cups water

½ cups red bean paste
1 cup sugar
4 tbsps cornstarch
⅓ cup white vegetable shortening or margarine
Pinch salt
½ tsp almond extract
2 tbsps sliced almonds

Place the dates in a large bowl and add the water. Cover loosely and cook 12-16 minutes on HIGH, or until the water boils and the dates begin to soften. Leave to stand 3 minutes. Drain the water from the dates and reserve 2 cups of the liquid and mix with the cornstarch, and cook 3-4 minutes on HIGH to

Facing page: Date and Red Bean Winter Pudding (top) and Jade Pieces (bottom). This page: Stuffed Lychees (left), Sweet Almond Pudding (center) and Agar-Agar Pudding (right).

thicken. Combine the dates, sugar, bean paste, shortening or margarine, salt and almond extract in a food processor and purée until smooth. Mix into the thickened date liquid and cook for 2 minutes on HIGH, stirring frequently. Pour into a serving bowl and chill. Sprinkle with almonds. May be served with cream if desired.

GLOSSARY

Agar-Agar This is a specially-prepared, dried seaweed which is sold in the shops as Chinese grass. The white, fibrous strands require soaking and are used like gelatine. Agar-agar is also sold in ground powder form. It is used for puddings and as a setting agent. All Chinese and Oriental food shops sell it.

Arrowroot The starchy extract of the ground root of an American plant, used as a thickening agent for sauces.

Bean Curd This comes in soft, custard-like squares and is made from soy beans. It is highly nutritious and is one of the most important Chinese foods. It is available only from Chinese grocers and is also sold in dried form as bean curd stick, in brine, and fried.

Bean Pastes Sauces made from soy beans which are sold in cans and jars. Once opened, they should be kept refrigerated. There are many varieties of bean paste:
Hot Bean Paste, which is made with chilies and is salty.
Soy Bean Paste, which is dark in color, very salty and is made with fermented soy beans.
Sweet Bean Paste, which is made with black soy beans, sugar, flour and spices.
Yellow Bean Paste, which is made with yellow soy beans and is also quite salty in taste.

Bean Sprouts These are shoots of mung beans or soy beans. The soy beans are stronger in flavor. They are readily available from most super-markets and Oriental shops. Fresh bean sprouts will keep for several days if refrigerated in a perforated plastic bag; discard any discolored shoots. The topped and tailed sprouts are known as 'Silver Sprouts' and are used for very special dishes.

Black Bean Sauce This can be bought ready-made from shops, or made with 3-4 tbsps steamed, black soy beans mixed to a paste with 2 tbsps oil and 2 tbsps sugar.

Broths Chinese cooking needs broth of one sort or another in almost all dishes. There are two main kinds of broth that are used. It is very useful to make home-made broth, which will keep refrigerated for 5-7 days. Alternatively, bouillon cubes can be substituted.

Chicken Broth 2lbs chicken trimmings (bones, neck, skin, wings, claws etc), 3½ pints water, 1 inch fresh root ginger, peeled and minced, 1 medium onion, peeled and thinly sliced, salt, freshly ground black pepper. Put chicken trimmings and water into a pan. Bring to the boil and simmer for 10 minutes. Skim and add ginger, onions and seasoning; simmer for 1-1½ hours. Strain and use.

Superior Broth or Strong Broth 1 boiling chicken, 4oz loin of pork, cubed, 1oz Yunnan ham, cubed, 3½ pints water, ½ inch fresh root ginger, peeled and thinly sliced, 2 green onions, chopped, salt, freshly ground black pepper. Place chicken, pork and ham into a pan with the water and bring to the boil. Cook for 10 minutes and skim. Add ginger, green onions and season with salt and pepper. Simmer for 1½ hours. The fat should not be skimmed off completely as this gives the stock its characteristic flavor.

Chili Oil This can be brought ready-prepared. Chili oil can also be made by infusing dried chilies in hot vegetable oil, but it will not keep for as long as the ready-prepared variety.

Chili Peppers There are numerous varieties of chili peppers, varying in size and strength of flavor. Commonly used in Eastern cooking are the red and green finger-like chili peppers, about 4 inches long, and the tiny red and green birds-eye chili peppers, which are very hot. When preparing chili peppers, it is advisable to wear rubber gloves and avoid getting the oils near the lips and eyes. The seeds, which are very hot, should be discarded unless a very fiery dish is desired.

Chili Powder Dried fruit pod of the capsicum plant, in flaked or powdered form. It is very hot and spicy, and should be purchased only in small quantities.

Chili Sauce This is a very hot, spicy and tangy sauce made from chilies and vinegar. Chili sauce can be purchased from many supermarkets and all Chinese grocers. It is used to season a wide variety of savory Chinese dishes.

Chinese Broccoli A dark green, leafy vegetable which bears small white flowers; it looks very much like miniature broccoli. It is sold only in Chinese grocers and, if not available, it can be substituted by Chinese cabbage or ordinary broccoli.

Chinese Cabbage There are two main varieties. One is called Pak-choy, and the other, a more tender flowering white cabbage, is called Choy-sum. Chinese leaves and Tiensin cabbage are sold in supermarkets and Oriental shops, and also in many fruit and vegetable markets. Chinese leaves are tightly packed and have creamy white leaves with a thick central stalk. They are often used in salads in place of lettuce. All these cabbages can be substituted by ordinary cabbage.

Chinese Dates These are sold in dried form and will keep for a month. There are two varieties: black and red, and they can be purchased from most Oriental shops. They resemble dried prunes and are used in sweet, and some savory, stir-fried dishes. Ordinary dried dates can easily be used in their place.

Chinese Parsley Otherwise known as fresh coriander, this is a herb of Indian origin, which is used as a flavoring and a garnish. The flat leaves have a strong flavor and cannot be substituted by Western parsley.

Chinese Wine There are many kinds of wine made from rice. Chinese rice wine can be substituted by ordinary dry sherry in most recipes. Rice wines vary considerably in quality, but they are all very strong.

Chives Now available in most parts of the world, these have a subtle onion taste and bright green stems which are used, snipped, as a garnish for soups and other dishes.

Cinnamon Delicate, sweet spice which is the dried, aromatic bark of a type of laurel. Cinnamon can be purchased in bark, quill or powdered form.

Cloud Ear This is known by many names i.e. wood ear, snow fungus, sea jelly or jelly sheet. It is actually a dried fungus which, when soaked in water, resembles a puffed ear, hence the name. It has no flavor and is used only to add texture to a dish. It will keep for about a month in its dried form.

Cloves The dried, aromatic buds of a type of myrtle native to Southeast Asia. Used whole, or with the central bud ground into a powder, cloves have preserving properties, and are used in both sweet and savoury dishes.

Cooked Oil Many Chinese dishes require the use of cooked oil. It is

made by heating vegetable, peanut or any other kind of oil until it smokes.

Cornstarch A fine, white maize flour used as a thickener, mainly for sauces.

Fennel (dried) This is sold in seed form and the tiny, pale green seeds resemble caraway seeds. Fennel is sold in supermarkets, health food shops and in Chinese grocery shops, and it is an important ingredient in five spice powder.

Five Spice Powder This is a strong, coffee-colored seasoning made with equal parts of finely-ground fagara (brown peppercorns), cinnamon bark, clove, fennel and star anise. Use sparingly.

Flour Many varieties of flour are used in Chinese cookery, the main one being the ordinary all-purpose type, which is usually a finely ground wheat flour. It is used to make most steamed breads and some pastries.
High Gluten Flour This is used to make wonton wrappers. It is a strong flour with a high gluten content and can therefore be rolled very thinly.
Tang Flour This is made from a low-gluten wheat. The flour is used for making clear wrappers for Dim Sum because, when cooked, this flour becomes transparent.

Ginger Fresh root ginger is a vital ingredient in Chinese cooking; nearly all the traditional meat and fish dishes use root ginger. Sprouting ginger is the best and it is used for preserving foods in vinegar and for pickling. The tough, older roots are strong in flavor. The texture may be fibrous, but if you chop the ginger finely with a sharp knife it will release its full flavor. Ginger not only gives a distinct taste to a dish but it helps the digestion as well. Fresh ginger cannot be substituted by ground or preserved ginger. It is widely available.

Glutinous Rice This is also known as 'sticky' rice. It is a special variety of Chinese rice which has opaque grains, and when cooked turns transparent and very sticky. It is used for making both desserts and savory dishes.

Hoisin Sauce This is a sweet, brownish-red sauce made from soy beans, salt, sugar, chili, garlic, vinegar and flour. It has a sweet, tangy flavor and can be bought from Chinese shops or large supermarkets. It is used in cooking as well as being served as a dip for meats etc. It is also known as seafood sauce or barbecue sauce.

Long Beans These are one of the many typical Chinese vegetables. As the name suggests, they are longer than ordinary beans. They are obtainable from most Chinese shops and from Oriental grocers and can be substituted by lobia beans or ordinary green beans.

Lotus Root is available canned or fresh from Chinese groceries. Cut in thin rounds, it has a flower-like appearance. Obtained from waterlilies. Seeds are available preserved or fresh at Chinese New Year, and reputedly bring good luck. Leaves are available from Chinese groceries to cook in or on. Should be soaked first.

Monosodium Glutamate This is a white, crystalline substance commonly known as MSG. It is used extensively in Chinese cookery for tenderising meat and for enhancing the flavor of dishes. It is sometimes sold under the names of Aji No Moto and Vi Tsin and is also called 'taste powder'. It should be used sparingly, as too much will spoil the dish, and can be totally omitted from recipes if preferred.

Mooli Mooli or muli is a crisp, white variety of radish. It grows to about 10 inches in length and 4 inches in diameter. It has a stronger taste than ordinary red radish and is eaten in salads and as a vegetable. It has a crunchy texture and a sharp flavor.

Mushrooms There are many varieties of dried mushrooms which are used in Chinese cooking. Follow the recipe to see the type suggested. To prepare dried mushrooms for cooking, soak in hot water for ½ hour. Drain and season with ½ tbsp wine and a little sugar. (See also Chinese Mushrooms and Cloud Ear.)

Mustard Green This is also known as leaf mustard. It has a slightly bitter taste and is crunchy in texture. It is used in soups and stir-fried dishes. It is only sold in Oriental and Chinese grocery shops. Use broccoli as the nearest substitute.

Noodles There are many different kinds of noodles. Some are made from wheat flour, some from rice flour and some from bean flour. All these varieties of noodles are obtainable from Chinese and Oriental grocers, and many are sold in supermarkets and other food shops. Noodles can be substituted by spaghetti, though the flavor will not be the same.
Bean Thread Noodles Thin, white, transparent noodles made from moong bean flour. They should be soaked before use.

Cake Noodles These are bound together in tight balls.
Rice Sheet Noodles These are made from rice and come in wide, flat sheets. They are also sold in dried form.
Rice Stick Noodles Sometimes called rice vermicelli, these are very thin noodles made from rice. They must be soaked in hot water for 10-12 minutes before use. If deep-fried they become very light and crisp, like wafers.
Shanghai Noodles, Thin These are mostly used in soups and are thin and pale in color. The basic noodles are made from wheat flour.
Shanghai Noodles, Thick These are yellowish in color and are made from wheat flour enriched with egg. Commonly sold in dried form in the shape of small and large cakes, they are also sold fresh in Chinese shops. Fresh noodles can be kept in plastic bags in the refrigerator for up to 1 week.

Oyster Sauce This is a special sauce produced from soy sauce and oysters which have been fermented together. It is used as a flavoring, coloring and also as a condiment. Once opened it will keep in the bottle for several months.

Pea Pods Also known as snow peas and mangetout, these are delicate, flat pea pods. The whole vegetable is eaten. They are either eaten raw or lightly cooked, and they add character and color to many dishes. Will keep for a few days if kept in perforated plastic bags in the refrigerator.

Preserved Chinese Vegetables These are specially prepared dried vegetables which retain their original flavor. Preserved vegetables are also sold in cans and jars, packed in a brine solution.

Rice There are many different varieties of rice. Long grained rice is the variety usually used for making simple rice dishes, but a special, glutinous, medium-grain rice is used for making desserts and savory dishes.

Sesame Oil An aromatic oil produced from sesame seeds. This has a special flavor and is used both as a seasoning and as a vital ingredient in some sauces. Sold in bottles, it is available from most general grocery and healthfood shops.

Soy Sauce There are two kinds of soy sauce; one is dark and the other is light. Made from fermented soy beans, both varieties are used for flavoring soups, stir-fried dishes and for seasoning nearly all Chinese foods. The dark soy sauce is thicker and stronger in flavor while the lighter varieties are the weaker infusions of the fermented beans. The first extract is the strongest and the best. Soy sauces are sometimes flavored with mushrooms, oysters and shrimp roe.

Star Anise This is an eight-pointed clove with a strong anise smell and flavor, and is one of the spices which goes into Chinese five spice powder. It can be purchased in powder or whole form. It is used to flavor red-cooked poultry and many meat dishes.

Tangerine Peel, Dried The best sun-dried peels are several years old. Peel is used as a seasoning for stews and other dishes. It is a little expensive, however, and can be omitted from the recipe, or substituted by home-dried peels.

Vinegar Chinese vinegars are made from fermented rice, by the process of distillation, and there are four main varieties:

Black Vinegar This is similar to malt vinegar, but not quite so strong. It has a stronger flavor than other Chinese varieties, and is used both as a flavoring and as a condiment.
Red Vinegar This is distinctly red in color as the name suggests, and is used particularly with seafood dishes and as a condiment.
Sweet Vinegar This is almost like port in flavor, very sweet and rich black in color. It is used mainly for braised and stewed dishes and has a sharp taste.
White Vinegar This is not as strong as European white vinegar; it is milder and more tangy. When substituting one vinegar for another, taste carefully.

Water Chestnuts These are the bulb-like stems of the bulrush. They are slightly sweet and have a crisp texture. They are usually sold in cans; occasionally they are sold in their natural form. They are available from some supermarkets and all Oriental and Chinese shops. Canned water chestnuts will keep for 3-4 weeks after opening if refrigerated and kept in water. The water should be changed daily. Chestnuts are also ground to a flour, which is used for making batter.

Winter Melon This is a very large, green-skinned melon with a soft, white flesh and a delicate taste. It is sold fresh in Chinese shops or Oriental grocers, but can also be purchased cubed in cans. Peeled and seeded marrow or cucumber can be used as a substitute.

Wonton Wrappers or Skins Very thin wrappers made from a mixture of wheat, eggs and water. These can be purchased ready-made, usually in 3-inch squares, or made at home.

Worcestershire Sauce A hot sauce containing malt vinegar, molasses, chili peppers, spices, anchovies and tropical fruits. It should be used sparingly.

Yunnan Ham This is a special kind of Chinese smoked ham which is produced by a salting and smoking process. Substitute: good cuts of European smoked ham, smoked gammon or lean rashers of smoked bacon.

INDEX

Agar-Agar Pudding 168
Almond Cookies 164
Asparagus Salad 142
Assorted Meat Congee 42
Bamboo Shoots with Green Vegetables 151
Bananas Cooked in Coconut Milk 164
Barbecued Pork 80
Bean Sprouts with Chopped Pork 108
Beans with Tree Ears and Bamboo Shoots 154
Beef and Oyster Sauce 80
Beef Steak with Ginger 88
Beef with Broccoli 68
Beef with Green Beans 98
Beef with Green Pepper and Chili 83
Beef with Green Pepper, Tomato and Black Beans 92
Beef with Mango 76
Beef with Pineapple and Peppers 70
Beef with Tree Ears 80
Beef Worcestershire 90
Boiled Shrimp 58
Braised Cauliflower with Chili 151
Braised Eggplant and Chicken with Chili 150
Braised Hong Kong Beef 98
Braised Pork with Spinach and Mushrooms 105
Calves' Liver with Piquant Sauce 100
Cantonese Lobster 56
Cantonese Shrimp 56
Chicken and Asparagus Soup 26

Chicken and Cashew Nuts 116
Chicken and Mushroom Soup 12
Chicken and Mushrooms 125
Chicken Chop Suey 130
Chicken Chow Mein 122
Chicken Corn Soup with Almonds 8
Chicken Curry 140
Chicken Fry with Sauce 124
Chicken Green Chili 133
Chicken Livers with Peppers 138
Chicken Noodle Soup 10
Chicken with Hoisin Sauce and Cashews 128
Chicken with Mango 132
Chicken with Pea Pods 128
Chili Oil Dip 148
Chili Sauce 149
Chili Shrimp 16
Chili Sichuan Chicken 136
Chinese Bean Buns 166
Chinese Combination Soup 18
Chinese Noodle Soup with Pork Dumplings 16
Chinese Parsley and Fish Soup 10
Corn and Chicken Soup 14
Corn and Crabmeat Soup 18
Crab and Sweet Corn Soup 28
Crab and Watercress Soup 26
Crab Rolls 24
Crabmeat Egg Foo Yung, Cantonese 56
Crispy Fish with Chili 62
Date and Red Bean Winter Pudding 169
Deep-Fried Crispy Chicken 130
Deep-Fried Noodles 42

Deep-Fried Pork Meatballs 108
Devilled Kidneys 100
Diced Chicken and Peppers 120
Diced Pork with Corn 74
Diced Pork with Walnuts 108
Duck Soup 10
Duck with Five Spices 140
Duck with Ginger and Pineapple 114
Duck with Onions 138
Duck with Orange 126
Duck with Pineapple 140
Dumpling Wrappers 44
Egg Drop Soup 24
Egg Fu Yung 32
Egg Noodles with Meat Sauce 44
Egg Pancakes with Filling 30
Eggflower Soup 20
Eight Precious Rice 42
Embroidered Crabmeat Balls 66
Empress Chicken 116
Fish in Wine Sauce 54
Fish Steamed on Lotus Leaves 54
Fish with Chicken and Vegetables 55
Fish with Vegetables and Bean Curd 54
Five-Spice Beef with Broccoli 111
Four Happiness Dumplings 16
Fried Bean Curd with Mushrooms 161
Fried Meat Dumplings 23
Fried Noodles with Shredded Chicken 41
Fried Rice Noodles 42
Fried Rice with Egg 38

Fried Shredded Chicken on Cabbage 116
Fried Vegetables with Ginger 161
Garlic Dip 148
Garlic Shrimp with Salt and Pepper 16
Ginger Broccoli 156
Ginger Dip 142
Ginger Sauce 156
Ginger Scallops in Oyster Sauce 64
Golden Chicken with Walnuts 116
Green Chili and Ginger Dip 144
Guy's Curry 111
Ham and Bean Fried Rice 32
Happys' Curry 94
Hoi Sin Sauce 149
Honey Sesame Shrimp 64
Honey Soy Chicken Wings 138
Hot and Sour Soup 10 and 26
Hot Mustard Sauce 152
Jade and Ivory Pork 74
Jade Pieces 168
Julienne of Vegetables 160
Kidneys with Bacon 106
Kung Pao Shrimp 52
Kung Pao Lamb 96
Lacquered Duck with Plum Sauce 126
Lamb Meatballs with Yogurt 88
Lamb with Cherries 106
Lamb with Tomatoes 102
Lemon Chicken 138
Lettuce and Bean Sprouts with Soy Sauce 149
Lion's Head 94
Mango Sauce 160
Marbled Eggs 42

Meat and Shrimp Chow Mein 30
Mixed Vegetables with Peanut Sauce 150
Mongolian Lamb with Onions 102
Noodles in Soup 30
Noodles with Beef and Almonds 43
Noodles with Pork and Shrimp 106
Noodles with Pork Fu Yung 40
Okra and Tomatoes 161
Pea Pods with Shrimp 63
Pea Pods with Water Chestnuts 142
Peking Duck with Pancakes 121
Peking Sweet Lamb 112
Pineapple Sauce 150
Pineapple Shrimp with Peppers 62
Pink and Silver Pork 76
Piquant Lambs' Livers 108
Plain Fried Rice 43
Plain Rice 34
Plum Sauce 142
Pork Chop Suey 88
Pork Chops, Shanghai Style 92
Pork Chow Mein 84
Pork in Plum Sauce with Almonds 76
Pork Meatballs in Sauce 79
Pork Spare Ribs 78
Pork with Black Bean Sauce 88
Pork with Chili 94
Pork with Green Pepper 84
Pork with Plum Sauce 86
Pork-Stuffed Mushrooms 72
Ratatouille 160
Red Bean Filled Dim Sums 166

Rice Noodles Singaporee Style 30
Rice Paper Shrimp Parcels 24
Rice Supreme 42
Rice with Ground Beef 44
Roast Crispy Duck 114
Roast Peking Duck 120
Roast Spiced Duck 118
Scallops in Pepper Sauce 56
Seafood Combination 50
Seafood Hot and Sour Soup 15
Sesame Beef with Dates 110
Sesame Chicken with Garlic Sauce 130
Sesame Crab in Asparagus Ring 51
Sesame Fried Chicken 140
Shanghai Noodle Snack 44
Shredded Beef with Vegetables 110
Shredded Pork with Preserved Vegetables 96
Shrimp and Cauliflower 63
Shrimp and Ginger 58
Shrimp and Lettuce Soup 28
Shrimp Egg Rice 36
Shrimp Fu Yung 36
Shrimp in Egg Custard 34
Shrimp in Hot Sauc 48
Shrimp Toast 28
Shrimp with Bean Curd 52
Shrimp with Broccoli 48
Shrimp with Cashew Nuts 60
Shrimp with Pea Pods and Corn 59
Shrimp with Peas 60
Singapore Chicken 134
Singapore Fried Noodles 46
Sizzling Rice or Singing Rice 34
Sliced Duck with Bamboo

Shoots 114
Sliced Pork in Wine Sauce 72
Soup of Mushrooms and Peas 10
Soy Dip 148
Special Fried Rice 156
Spiced Beef 83
Spiced Liver 98
Spicy Cucumbers 154
Spinach, Chinese Style 157
Spring Roll Wrappers 20
Spring Rolls (Egg Rolls) 28
Spring Rolls 22
Squid with Broccoli and Cauliflower 66
Squid with Shrimp and Tomatoes 66
Steak Chinese Style 70
Steak with Black Bean Sauce 104
Steak with Peanut Sauce 104
Steamed Barbecued Pork Dumplings 24
Steamed Beef Balls with Two Different Mushrooms 80
Steamed Beef Szechuan Style 82
Steamed Chicken 130
Steamed Chicken Wontons 24

Steamed Crabmeat and Egg Custard 20
Steamed Custard 164
Steamed Duck in Wine Sauce 119
Steamed Eggplant 142
Steamed Fish in Ginger 64
Steamed Fish with Black Beans 48
Steamed Shrimp Pancakes 12
Steamed Lamb with Mushroom Sauce 102
Steamed Open Dumplings 12
Steamed Pork with Salted Cabbage 82
Stewed Chicken and Pineapple 122
Stir-Fried Beef with Onions 110
Stir-Fried Chicken with Yellow Bean Paste 132
Stir-Fried Eggs with Shredded Meats and Vegetables 40
Stir-Fried Shanghai Noodles 44
Stir-Fried Vegetable Medley 157
Stuffed Lychees 168
Stuffed Mushrooms with Pork and Water Chestnuts 8
Subgum Fried Rice 38
Sweet Almond Pudding 168

Sweet and Sour Beef 103
Sweet and Sour Cabbage 148
Sweet and Sour Chicken 122
Sweet and Sour Fish 46
Sweet and Sour Pork 97
Sweet and Sour Pork and Pineapple 68
Sweet and Sour Pork with Peppers 90
Sweet and Sour Sauce 160
Sweet and Sour Shrimp 52
Sweet Dumpling 164
Sweet-Sour Cabbage 146
Szechuan Beef 110
Szechuan Eggplant 144
Tangerine Peel Chicken 122
Ten Varieties of Beauty 160
Tossed Noodles 36
Vegetable Rice 41
Velvet Noodles 36
Wok Sweet and Sour Cabbage 154
Wonton Soup 12
Wonton Wrappers 20
Wontons with Pork and Shrimp Filling 22
Yang Chow Fried Rice 158